Christian M...

Pass The Salt

America ASLEEP kNOw MORE

Where Are Our Shepherds?

Disobedience, pride, greed, fear,

and silence of the shepherds are causing the

loss of lives and the souls of our children

For More Information Contact

America ASLEEP kNOw MORE

P.O. Box 130

Humansville, MO 65674

www.asleepknowmore.com

Dr. Gregory Thompson

WHERE ARE OUR SHEPHERDS?

Published by Viewpoint Press
Springfield, Missouri U.S.A.
Printed in U.S.A.

Viewpoint Press is an evangelical Christian publisher dedicated to serving the local church with purpose books. We believe God's vision for 21st Century Press is to provide church leaders with biblical, user- friendly materials that will help them evangelize, disciple and minister to children, youth and families.

Viewpoint Press
2131 W. Republic Rd. PMB 41
Springfield, MO 65807

www.21stcenturypress.com

800-658-0284

Cover Design: Lee Fredrickson
ISBN 978-0-9766243-2-5

MAKE YOUR VIEWS PUBLIC!

DEDICATION

First to Coach Dave Daubenmire a best friend to Jesus, and thus a best friend to me, for agreeing to co-author this book, and with his great gift from God in the oral and written word, make this a better offering than it would otherwise be to our Lord and Savior Jesus Christ, and to HIS children for who it is written. Coach, also for your steadfast boldness to stand at great personal cost as you have denied yourself and picked up your cross for Christ. My dad and brothers, what a joy that God put you in my life to guide and strengthen me. Other servant warriors that have come forward in their life to speak the truth included in this book: Pope John Paul II, Dr. Alan Keyes, Pastor Flip Benham, Pastor Joe Larson, Father Corapi, Pastor Ernie Sanders, Pastor Mark Kiser, Pastor David Wilkerson, Pastor Bill Dunfee, Pastor R.L. Beasley, Mark Cahill, Randall Terry, James Hartline, Steve Klein, Adam Tenant, David Tremble, Dee Wampler, and other friends of Jesus I may have failed to mention.

Imitating Christ's Humility is the type of men that God has placed into my path, men that have been wretched in their lives, men that have sinned, men that have repented, men that seek to serve the Lord. Pray for them as they try to imitate Christ and that in their mind, on their lips, and in their hearts they are faithful to God's will. Give them the wisdom and humility as stated in Philippians 2:

"If you have any encouragement from being united with Christ, if any comfort from his love, if any fellowship with the Spirit, if any tenderness and compassion, then make my joy complete by being like-minded, having the same love, being one in spirit and purpose. Do nothing out of selfish ambition or vain conceit, but in humility consider others better than yourselves. Each of you should look not only to your own interests, but also to the interests of others. Your attitude should be the same as that of Christ Jesus: Who, being in very nature God, did not consider equality with God something to be grasped, but made himself nothing, taking the very nature of a servant, being made in human likeness. And being found in appearance as a man, he humbled himself and became obedient to death— even death on a cross!

Therefore God exalted him to the highest place and gave him the name that is above every name, that at the name of Jesus every knee should bow, in heaven and on earth and under the earth, and every tongue confess that Jesus Christ is Lord, to the glory of God the Father."

Though the men mentioned above, know that they are unworthy to carry the shoes of Jesus, I thank God that He put them into the path of my life to encourage and counsel me in different ways, but always on the path to eternity with Jesus.

TABLE OF CONTENTS

1. Bear Witness to the Truth:..15

2. Christian Pimps 20

3. Letter to Fr. David Tyson, Superior to Fr. Jenkins...............25

4. Hired Shepherds 41

5. The Shepherds Are Sleeping 46

6. Must I Tear Away the Limb that is Bound?.........................51

7. Sheep Without Shepherds 55

8. Church Militant at Notre Dame...63

9. What Does It Mean to be a Pro-Life Christian?..................67

10. The Congregation of the Dead (No Shepherds?)..................74

11. Fear, Pride, and Greed 77

12. A Subtle Sin—Easy to Ignore..81

13. Are Christians Helping Send Children to Hell?..................84

14. What Does Abortion, Homosexuality, and Islam Have in Common?..87

15. America Was Founded Upon the Principles of Christianity.................89

16. Do You attend a State Controlled Church? 91

17. Jesus is God..94

18. Nose Wipers 97

19. What Have You Done?..102

20. Pornography is Dangerous 105

21. Why Graphic Signs?...107

22. Black Regiment..111

23. Take the Muzzle Off...113

24. Light a Fire Under Your Pastor..117

25. Act…Contend! 121

26. The Time is Now! 123

27. Armed but not Dangerous vs. Dangerous but not Armed 125

28. Correction of Modern Day Preachers..............................127

29. The Church Isn't Ready for Revival! 131

30. They Hated Him Without a Cause....................................148

31. Woe to Self Serving Disobedience....................................156

32. "Teacher What Good Must I Do…?"................................160

33. The Counterfeit Gospel is Real!..162

34. Willful Ignorance..169

35. Where are the Prophets?..175

FOREWORD

"The grass withers, and the flowers fade, but the word of God stands forever" (Isaiah 40:8).

Understand this right now, stop and pray that you understand what I am about to tell you. It is so important that you repent and pray that you will be humble. It is hard for many and for many different reasons. For a Shepherd it can be a thorn in the side, for a servant warrior for the Lord it can make his warrior attributes with little or no effect, the power of God will not be with the proud. Humility must be one of the greatest attributes of the warriors for God. God will use the humble, but each of you have to understand that pride is an abomination to God. To the Shepherd and the Warrior, or blessed be the day when the two are one, as long as it is in humility and seeking to honor and glorify God. You have heard it said, "Pride goes before the fall," and to paraphrase Paul, you can be right, but at the same time very wrong in the eyes of God, if you do not lead all things with love and forgiveness. Also, understand that the words in the pages of this book can cause a strong reaction

May each of our brothers that are ignorant, or weak in any way, by the grace of God understand the beauty and love of the chastisement within these pages. May I someday join each person that will feel offended with the truth in the pages that follow, committed to Jesus, and placed in the hands of God, who is our refuge and our strength. Remember those that have a warrior spirit and will feel a carnal pull toward pride, need to remember your wretchedness in the eyes of God up to the point of your second birth, and that you do nothing of any good toward man that is not a gift of grace from God. Let the words of Mary ring in your ears as you go forward in this book, "this is my son, do what he says."

Bottom line, pray, stand, and act. And when you do anything, do it to honor and glorify the Lord, always seeking that HIS will be done.

This book is written to bear witness to the Truth, to give honor and glory to God. Our LORD and Savior Jesus Christ wishes that none would perish, may you have eyes to see and ears to hear His Truth. WOE!!! To the Shepherds and people that call themselves Christian, that do what is right in their own eyes.

"Then spake Jesus again unto them, saying, I am the light of the world: he that follows me shall not walk in darkness, but shall have the light of life" (John 8:12).

"For God, who commanded the light to shine out of darkness, hath shined in our hearts, to give the light of the knowledge of the glory of God in the face of Jesus Christ" (2 Corinthians 4:6).

"This is the condemnation, that light is come into the world, and men loved darkness rather than light, because their deeds were evil" (John 3:19).

"Woe unto them that call evil good, and good evil; that put darkness for light, and light for darkness; that put bitter for sweet, and sweet for bitter" (Isaiah 5:20).

Light is Truth, darkness is a lie, and so we have a battle between the Truth and a Lie, the light and darkness, the good and the evil, in this book you will see HIS Truth, and you will see how many Shepherds have fallen from the Truth to a lie, and need much prayer, not only for their souls, but for the sheep in their care.

"Be still, and know that I am God: I will be exalted among the heathen, I will be exalted in the earth. The LORD of hosts is with us; the God of Jacob is our refuge" (Psalm 46:10-11).

The fact is, you are going to die! What then? Many will spend eternity in hell because the Shepherds in the Church did not speak up.

Pray with me: Most gracious Heavenly Father, we cry out for the faithfulness of the Shepherds to return and be like the faithfulness of Christ. May the Holy Spirit give them the strength to separate again from the world so that they serve you by tending your sheep. The Children are dying and losing their souls because of the lack of true Shepherds, turn the Shepherds back to a valiant faith that can face the confusion and conflict. Father give your Shepherds strength to overcome temptations and help them to return to fidelity in you. May those that Shepherd have self sacrifice and a denial of self as you protect them from evil. Let the Shepherds pick up their cross and again follow you. May the light of your Truth shine through their lives and return them to good works as defined by you, not man. They have but human hearts with human frailty, and have been weak in times of trouble and sorrow. In thought, word, and deed, give them a desire and your Grace to steadily grow in holiness. Increase their wisdom, knowledge, and understanding of your Truth. Let your will be done in their lives, so that your sheep are protected.

Loving Father, I plead for the above prayer to be answered, and that the Shepherds follow your will. But if they do not, I cry out for the lost lives and lost souls that the Shepherds are not making a stand to protect, and if they do not follow your ways, if they are disobedient, or greedy, or prideful, or fearful of man, or silent, aiding Satan in the moral decay, corruption, and death of our posterity, then like King David, I ask you to eliminate these enemies, make their wives widows, and their children fatherless.

I know that some of you may be indignant, saying "how can any Christian pray like David did." Can I ask, what are you willing to do to protect your loved ones? Would you stand in harm's way for the lives and souls of your family, friends, and neighbors? Would you use whatever force you could muster to protect them and their eternal souls? Who would you cry out to if they held you bound, tortured and killed your son in front of you, then raped and killed your wife and daughters, with one of your daughters not saved? Would you have an imprecatory prayer like David? Well these things are happening, and worse, because of the leadership inside and outside of the church. I had a family member tortured and murdered, and while I have forgiven and prayed for those responsible, I serve the King of Kings and His children I am to warn and protect. Like Jesus said, I forgive, and pray for the souls of the people responsible, even as I cry out to Him with the blood of my grandson, to turn their hearts, or bring judgment to stop the loss of lives and souls.

Understand, knowing the Truth is important for you? Understand, your actions make a difference? We are at WAR for the lives and souls of the children, and no matter what rhetoric is used to distract you to other compassionate issues, if we do not address these things first, we dishonor God and He will never bless us or our nation.

Rev. Charles Finney said it very well, "If there is a decay of conscience, the pulpit is responsible for it. If the public press lacks moral discernment, the pulpit is responsible for it. If the church is denigrate and worldly, the pulpit is responsible for it. If the world loses its interest in Christianity, the pulpit is responsible for it. If Satan rules in our halls of legislation, the pulpit is responsible for it. If our politics become so corrupt that the very foundations of our government are ready to fall, the pulpit is responsible for it."

Shepherds do not love you if they did not tell you the Truth of God, just so your feelings would not be hurt, and you ended up in hell for eternity, what kind of love would that be? With love and forgiveness we come following our Teacher, who said, "Repent for the kingdom of heaven is at hand."

Like Paul said to the Galatians, "Have I now become your enemy because I am telling you the truth?" They killed Jesus for telling the Truth, they killed the Apostles for telling the Truth, they killed the prophets for telling the

Truth. Many Christians are being killed or imprisoned today for telling the Truth. Lord, that I may carry you on my back, like the donkey who had that great honor, and may I always speak your Truth with boldness, where ever that may take me.

Listen to the wisdom of Solomon, "Whatever you do, do it with all of your might, for there will be no work, or planning, or knowledge, or wisdom, in the grave, where you are going." Did I mention that you are going to die? What then?

This book is about so much more than Notre Dame, but know that Notre Dame is culpable in helping to destroy the nation, and the lives and souls of Christian children. It is so much more than President Barry, aka. Obama, and the atheistic communists in the Democratic Party. It is so much more than pagans like Romney and the other useless idiots in the Republican Party. It is so much more than the murdering of babies by both parties. It is so much more than the promotion of Sodomy by both parties. It is so much more than the Pagan lie from the pit of hell called Islam, supported by both parties. It is so much more than the Masons, Knights of Columbus, and others that hide within Christian ranks with blood on their hands. It is so much more than the hirelings and Pharisees within Focus on the Family, AFA, ACLJ, and many other Christian organizations, it is so much more than the silent educators in this country, especially the ones that are part of the atheistic communist N.E.A., and many college professors. It will put the shame and sin squarely on the dupes of Satan, if I may, the ones that are in the Shepherd, Teacher, and Master roles within the Christian church today. Each of these groups seek a seat at the table with the Creator, and yet many of them are still like Judas, who listened to the same words from Jesus: "The Truth is, one of you will betray me." And yes, each of you will say like the apostles, "I'm not the one, am I, Lord? To which Jesus will say to many, "One of you who is eating with me now will betray me. For I, the Son of Man, must die, as the Scriptures declared long ago. But how terrible it will be for my betrayer. Far better for him if he had never been born!"

And what did Judas receive for betraying the King of Kings:
> Then one of the twelve, called Judas Iscariot went to the chief priests and said, "What are you willing to give me if I deliver Him to you?" And they counted out to him thirty pieces of silver. So from that time he sought opportunity to betray Him. WAR! Warriors needed for the battles now being engaged in for the lives of the children.

Warriors needed for the battles now being engaged in for the souls of the children. You and your family are not safe, anywhere, except God's presence. Who is at fault, and what can be done? Is God taking His hand away from protecting your nation because of you? I had a friend once say, "that silence is not golden, it is yellow," so cowards that don't want to know the truth, or start speaking the truth, and acting on the truth, might want to run at this point, continue in your personal disobedience and silence that puts blood on your hands. Sadly, many with blood on their hands are in the government, and the education system, but the greatest sadness is that the children are murdered, indoctrinated in evil, and put at risk for eternity because of the Shepherds and intellectuals within the church that, with pride, have a walk indicating they are smarter than God. "WOE unto them that call EVIL good, and good EVIL" (Isaiah 5:20).

"In a time of universal deceit, telling the TRUTH, is a revolutionary act."
—George Orwell

This book is not focusing on the fact that there are no Christians within the Democratic Party leadership in Washington D.C. and many parts of the country. They have blood on their hands, and are led by a mass murderer (Obama), that feels like he has been endorsed to spread the murder worldwide. They promote abominations all the way to the White House, led by a Pedophile that seeks to get rid of the elderly useless eaters. We are led by traitorous reprobates in the Democratic party, seeking to lead us with atheistic communism. We are at War, and Obama, Pelosi, Reid, Biden, etc., are traitors to God and the people. This book is not focusing on the fact that there are few if any true Christians in the Republican Party leadership in Washington D.C. and many parts of the country. They compromise with evil with the best of them, and thus by actions and silence allow abominations against God and the people, all the time smiling, while stabbing people in the backs. I ask you, what have they done historically to traitors during war, that are causing the loss of lives and souls of the people?

This book is about the failure of those in positions of Shepherds, who have failed to follow the teaching of the One True Shepherd, being more like Pilate than Jesus. Jesus told Pilate, "My kingdom does not belong to this world. If my kingdom were of this world, my subjects would be fighting to save me from being handed over to the Jews. As it is, my kingdom is not here." At

11

this Pilate (Shepherds today) said to him, "So, then, you are a king?" Jesus replied; "it is you who say I am a king. The reason I was born, the reason why I came into the world, is to testify to the truth. Anyone committed to the truth hears my voice." More and more of us and our children, because of the Shepherds and the Notre Dames, are replying just as Pilate did to Jesus' words. "Truth!" said Pilate, (Christian Shepherds, and many of the Christian schools and colleges, like Notre Dame,)

"What does that mean?"

If you are a Shepherd, like a pastor, priest, elder, teacher, Christian School or church board member, deacon, or etc., please listen for a change and act with courage, to what Jesus said, *All power is given unto Me in heaven and earth. Go you therefore, and teach all nations, baptizing them in the name of the Father, and of the Son, and of the Holy Ghost: Teaching them to observe all things whatsoever I have commanded you: and, lo, I am with you always, even unto the end of the world"* (Matthew 28:18-20).

Now, what are you waiting for? To know this, how does it hold that Christians and Shepherds do nothing? You might say, what do you mean, do nothing? We send some money to the missionaries, we have wonderful committee meetings, we give food to the local pantry, we help the widows and orphans, and we are involved in all the mercy ministries. First of all, do not neglect these things, yet there are lives and souls perishing, and to know what to do and not do it, is it not said to be a sin by God? As childrens souls are at risk of going to hell for eternity and children are murdered daily, do you think it will be a good idea to hang on to the thought that you will tell Jesus you fed the hungry, clothed the naked, while children went to hell? Will Jesus tell many Shepherds and sleeping Christians because of the Shepherds, to go over with the goats, that He does not know you?

I judge none of your hearts. Jesus has given me a gift to love you, but you must judge yourself, before Jesus does. I do judge out of love, your actions or lack of. Look around you; do you not understand the times at all? Are you willing to hear a prophetic warning, or do you just want your best life now? Do you want the truth, or just to feel good?

Get this book to every Shepherd of God's children, and every Christian, and give us feedback, if you heard His voice, or if you find a challenge with this writing, or you just need prayer for the strength to do what is right, call us, (Coach Dave 740-507-3211 or Dr. T. 417-894-5768) and may the Lord increase your wisdom, knowledge, and understanding of His Word and the times we live in.

Put things in order; seek first HIS kingdom and HIS righteousness, and all these things will be given to you as well. Open your ears and hearts to the following truth.

"It is impossible to further the common good without acknowledging and defending the right to life, upon which all the other inalienable rights of individuals are founded and from which they develop... Only respect for life can be the foundation and guarantee of the most precious and essential goods of society, such as democracy and peace" (John Paul II, Evangelium Vitae 101).

"Laws which authorize and promote abortion and euthanasia are therefore radically opposed not only to the good of the individual but also to the common good; as such they are completely lacking in authentic juridical validity. Disregard for the right to life, precisely because it leads to the killing of the person whom society exists to serve, is what most directly conflicts with the possibility of achieving the common good" (John Paul II, Evangelium Vitae 72).

Prayer should be our first response in any crisis. Don't wait until things are hopeless. Pray daily for God's guidance. Our problems are God's opportunities.

As long as the tiniest spark remains, a fire can be rekindled and fanned into a roaring blaze. Similarly, if just the smallest remnant of true believers retains the spark of faith, God can rebuild it into a strong nation. And if only a glimmer of faith remains in our hearts, God can use it to restore blazing faith in that believer. If you feel that only a spark of faith remains in you, ask God to use it to rekindle a blazing fire of commitment to Him.

We have become a nation where good Christian men and women are forced to choose between their country and their faith, because the Shepherds have failed miserably to protect.

Our Lord and Savior Jesus Christ commands us to be ever-watchful for His return, and ever-mindful that we have no lasting place on earth. When we have in our spirit a heavenly orientation, we can have true happiness in this world, recognizing the rewards of heaven have no proportion to the light sacrifices of life. Come Lord Jesus, Come.

As the times become darker and more dangerous, Christians must have hope and confidence, that God has never abandoned His people, and indeed, He never will.

Father in heaven, I come to you in a moment of time where the two of us can sit and talk together. I have some questions to ask, and I cry out to you for the souls of family and friends, that they can know you and love you even more than me, even as I ask to know and love you more daily. So many souls are going to hell, as so many men think that they know better than you, Father what can I do to serve you more, to empty myself more for you, to make every word, every thought, every action about you. The Shepherds have much Pride, believing they know more than you, and leading the sheep away, yet I have no excuse. The Shepherds have been Disobedient, causing the sheep to be devoured, yet I have no excuse. The Shepherds have been Greedy, sidestepping the truth, so not to cause anyone to quit coming in and adding to their business and pleasure, yet I have no excuse. The Shepherds have been fearful of man, without the fear of God, allowing wolves to come in and scatter the flock, yet I have no excuse. The Shepherds have been silent as many are killed by sacrifice to Molach, and souls are at risk of hell by government indoctrination, yet I have no excuse. God has called me to warn HIS children, and I have no excuse.

The word of the LORD came to me: "Son of man, prophesy against the shepherds of Israel (America); prophesy and say to them: 'This is what the Sovereign LORD says: Woe to the shepherds of Israel (America) who only take care of themselves! Should not shepherds take care of the flock? You eat the curds, clothe yourselves with the wool and slaughter the choice animals, but you do not take care of the flock. You have not strengthened the weak or healed the sick or bound up the injured. You have not brought back the strays or searched for the lost. You have ruled them harshly and brutally (by sending them on a modern course to hell). So they were scattered because there was no shepherd, and when they were scattered they became food for all the wild animals. My sheep wandered over all the mountains and on every high hill. They were scattered over the whole earth, and no one searched or looked for them.

" 'Therefore, you shepherds, hear the word of the LORD: As surely as I live, declares the Sovereign LORD, because my flock lacks a shepherd and so has been plundered and has become food for all the wild animals, and because my shepherds did not search for my flock but cared for themselves rather than for my flock, therefore, O shepherds, hear the word of the LORD: This is what the Sovereign LORD says: I am against the shepherds and will hold them accountable for my flock. I will remove them from tending the flock so that the shepherds can no longer feed themselves. I will rescue my flock from their mouths, and it will no longer be food for them" (Ezekial 34:1-10).

1

BEAR WITNESS TO THE TRUTH: AN UNEQUIVOCAL MORAL OBLIGATION FOR ALL CHRISTIANS.

What are you doing here, if you haven't read the Forward to this book? Did you start with prayer, and then read the forward to outline the direction we are going and why? Did you ask forgiveness of every thought, word, and deed that you have committed that would displease God? Did you ask the Holy Spirit to guide your steps? Did you put on the full armor of God? Do you love the ones in your care so much that you want to be used to help lead them to heaven? Now get back there and start things out right, and I will be praying for your journey through these pages that hopefully will help you see and hear what it is Jesus wants you to do. Take things personal that He is calling you to get things right by doing it His way, and let Jesus be Lord of your life, humble yourself, and let us begin.

Whether your personal character, boldness, fortitude, and courage can actually demonstrate what you have been given the grace to know to be true is another issue altogether. I will paraphrase Father John Corapi in this very important Truth for Christians. "Every Christian, faithful to the Gospel, has the moral obligation to bear witness to the truth, 'in season and out of season, convenient or inconvenient,' accepted or rejected. This mandate is nothing new of course, It's as old as the Old Testament, and as new as the New Testament. Nonetheless, I'm afraid that it has become more necessary than ever to remind ourselves of it."

Jesus told Pilate, "My kingdom does not belong to this world. If my kingdom were of this world, my subjects would be fighting to save me from being handed over to the Jews. As it is, my kingdom is not here." At this Pilate said to him, "So, then, you are a king?"

Jesus replied; "It is you who say I am a king. The reason I was born, the reason why I came into the world, is to testify to the truth. Anyone committed to the truth hears my voice.

More and more of us and our children are replying just as Pilate did to Jesus' words. "Truth!" said, "What does that mean?"

This is happening because of the teachings we are receiving from the pulpits, from shepherds who evidently are not committed to the truth, and do not hear the voice of Jesus. These are pulpits that have no true Shepherd. Parents, this does not let us of the hook. Scripturally, we are told that we are to study to show ourselves approved. Why are we told this? We are told this so that we may know God and what He wills for us. Pilate's words, "Truth, What does that mean?" is what the children come out of the government education system with, and as a result, our children are abused and their spirits tainted before they leave middle school in the Government school system. Yet the decay is even greater today, as the reach to destroy the lives and souls of the children has also infiltrated into the Christian schools and seminaries who put out defective Shepherds.

Again, Rev. Father John Corapi shines light on "the recent travesty involving the University of Notre Dame's invitation to the President of the United States (author's note, Scripturally this President is an enemy to God, family, and country) to give the commencement address and receive an honorary doctor of laws degree is the antithesis of Christian witness to the truth. Obama, a lawyer who vigorously, publicly, and consistently supports an anti-life and anti-family litany of evils will now receive an honorary doctor of laws degree..."

Obama, did indeed receive this degree, as an open worker of iniquity, (remember that God said He hates workers of iniquity.) a sinner in the eyes of all Christians that hear the voice of Jesus and are committed to the Truth. With blood on His hands, and leading the children's souls away from God we allowed evil darkness from an anti-Christ (Obama) to come into a place that once stood for and tried to send light into the world. Now, like the government schools, where darkness is taught to the children, many Christian schools have started to follow the call of Belial.

Obama and the ilk of both parties in Washington D.C. have blood on their hands and are putting millions at risk for eternity. The Shepherds, because of their silence, pride, fear, greed, and disobedience are culpable and need to pray for forgiveness and begin to stand and lead like God's MEN, and not like Satan's males.

Professing Truth with some words by Rev. Father Corapi, "...the obligation to bear witness to the truth weighs more heavily than ever to each one of us. We have rapidly entered into a new era of persecution of the Church and the Truth that she professes and teaches, reminding us again, 'The disciple of Christ must not only keep the faith and live by it, but also profess it, confidently bear witness to it, and spread it: All however must be prepared to confess Christ before men and to follow Him along the way of the Cross, amidst the persecutions which the Church never lacks.'" "So everyone who acknowledges me before men, I also will acknowledge before my Father who is in heaven; but whoever denies me before men, I also will deny before my father who is in heaven" (Matt. 10:32,33).

Shepherds, please pay attention: I will ask again, with the love and forgiveness of Jesus, caring what happens to the children, families, and YOU. "Would you knowingly give aid and comfort to any enemy determined to hurt, kill, and enslave you and everyone that you love and know? Or, worse yet, would you sit back in silence and let anyone put the children at risk of going to hell for eternity?" It takes more than a sermon. Take action.

All of you will soon be DEAD, and some may even take their last heartbeat by morning, what then? Shame on you if you think that you are wise in man's ways, for that is foolishness to God. Don't be distracted by those things that will come in front of you that have nothing to do with eternity.

False Teachers and Their Destruction

But there were also false prophets among the people, just as there will be false teachers among you. They will secretly introduce destructive heresies, even denying the sovereign Lord who bought them—bringing swift destruction on themselves. Many will follow their shameful ways and will bring the way of truth into disrepute. In their greed these teachers will exploit you with stories they have made up. Their condemnation has long been hanging over them, and their destruction has not been sleeping.

For if God did not spare angels when they sinned, but sent them to hell, putting them into gloomy dungeons to be held for judgment; if he did not spare the ancient world when He brought the flood on its ungodly people, but protected Noah, a preacher of righteousness, and seven others; if He condemned the cities of Sodom and Gomorrah by burning them to ashes, and made them an example of what is going to happen to the ungodly; and if He rescued Lot, a righteous man, who was distressed by the filthy lives of lawless men (for that righteous man, living among them day after day, was tormented in his righteous soul by the lawless deeds he saw and heard)— if this is so, then the Lord knows how to rescue godly men from trials and to hold the unrighteous for the day of judgment, while continuing their punishment. This is especially true of those who follow the corrupt desire of the sinful nature and despise authority.

Bold and arrogant, these men are not afraid to slander celestial beings; yet even angels, although they are stronger and more powerful, do not bring slanderous accusations against such beings in the presence of the Lord. But these men blaspheme in matters they do not understand. They are like brute beasts, creatures of instinct, born only to be caught and destroyed, and like beasts they too will perish.

Shepherds Listen: "They will be paid back with harm for the harm they have done. Their idea of pleasure is to carouse in broad daylight. They are blots and blemishes, reveling in their pleasures while they feast with you. With eyes full of adultery, they never stop sinning; they seduce the unstable; they are experts in greed—an accursed brood! They have left the straight-way and wandered off to follow the way of Balaam son of Beor, who loved the wages of wickedness. But he was rebuked for his wrongdoing by a donkey—a beast without speech—who spoke with a man's voice and restrained the prophet's madness.

These men (Shepherds) are springs without water and mists driven by a storm. Blackest darkness is reserved for them. For they mouth empty, boastful words and, by appealing to the lustful desires of sinful human nature, they entice people who are just escaping from those who live in error. They promise them freedom, while they themselves are slaves of depravity—for a man is a slave to whatever has mastered him. If they have escaped the corruption of the world by knowing our Lord and Savior Jesus Christ and are again entangled in it and overcome, they are worse off at the end than they were at the beginning. It would have been better for them not to have known the way of righteousness, than to have known it and then to turn their backs on the sacred command that was passed on to them. Of them the proverbs are true: "A dog returns to its vomit," and, "A sow that is washed goes back to her wallowing in the mud" (2 Peter 2:1-22).

I was crying out to my Father in heaven daily, not understanding why there was not any leadership from those that were looked upon as "Shepherds." There was so much loss of innocent life, so many souls at risk for eternity, because of the Shepherds being hearers and not doers of the word. Then the Lord prompted me to go to Notre Dame, and as a result of that SCANDAL to Christianity and especially the Catholic Church. This attempt to continue to warn the children of God, and speak the Truth was given life. There, God's intimate involvement brought into my presence Fr. Weslin, who seemed to me a "walking saint," someone who had been fasting for over thirty years, and had been arrested ninety plus times, who had broken bones by law enforcement, and many other sufferings for our Lord and Savior Jesus Christ and the innocent lives of the unborn. It was a great blessing to be able to carry a Cross with Fr. Weslin, and to go with him into jail for Jesus and the innocent, all because of what Satan's children, Fr. Jenkins and the board of Notre Dame were willing to do against our Lord and Savior Jesus Christ, and His mother Mary, who they were showing disrespect and spitting in her face. A great shame is on all who were involved in this scandal, which included many disobedient clergy, who can rationalize with the best of sinners, and to any donors that would continue to give aid and comfort to an institution that has become of the world, and threatens the souls of many of God's children.

Woe is you, Notre Dame, and any in the church that would endorse you, you are but a whitewashed tomb full of dead men's bones, home to a brood of vipers. Coach Dave and Dr. Alan Keyes are two valiant warriors for Jesus and all that Jesus stands for, which indeed begins with God's Truth and love. The Truth is surrounded by lies at Notre Dame, because of the Shepherds, but it is much bigger than just Notre Dame. Please give your love and prayers for Notre Dame's leadership, and all others that are at risk of hell for eternity.

2

CHRISTIAN PIMPS

"Christianity started in Palestine as a fellowship; it moved to Greece and became a philosophy; it moved to Italy and became an institution; it moved to Europe and became a culture; it came to America and became an enterprise." -Sam Pascoe

"An enterprise. That's a business." After a few moments Martha, the youngest student in the class, raised her hand. I could not imagine what her question might be. I thought the little vignette was self-explanatory, and that I had performed it brilliantly. Nevertheless, I acknowledged Martha's raised hand, "Yes, Martha." She asked such a simple question, "A business? But isn't it supposed to be a body?" I could not envision where this line of questioning was going, and the only response I could think of was, "Yes." She continued, "But when a body becomes a business, isn't that a prostitute?" as told by David Ryser (Authors note: Notre Dame and the Shepherds listen up)

I've been fighting for a long time the prompting of my inner man to take on this subject. Although I have chewed around the edges like I used to do as a child when I would break off the crust from a hot, home-made apple pie in attempt to appease my hunger without my mother finding out, I never really stuck my thumb into the middle of the pie.

I have been a sellout. A pimp, if you will. Not on purpose. It is easy to justify our lack of courage when confronted with difficult issues. I try to faithfully deliver the mail as the Lord hands it to me, but I have been negligent by eating the crust out of fear of spoiling the pie.

You see, I have pulled my punches. I have softened the blow. I have spanked with a newspaper when they deserved a belt. I have sold out on the Truth. I have not called a spade a spade. I have nibbled at the crust when I should have been hammering the pie. I have taken the be-nice approach and have listened to the "touch not God's anointed" mentality. I have prostituted the Truth. For that I am sorry.

Oh, my intentions were good. I had hoped that as I exposed the "unfruitful works of darkness" that the churches would eventually awaken and begin to push back against the enemy. After ten years of trying to awaken "The Church" to the problem I have finally mustered the courage to say what I have known all along. "The Church" IS the problem. It has become a pimp, selling the works of "the body" for personal satisfaction. Most of the pulpits are filled by "hirelings" (more on that in a future commentary), men and women who stand in the pulpit without a calling, without an anointing, and without courage. They are man pleasers, living off of "the Body" as they sell it out for their own whims and pleasures. Greedy Dogs, Isaiah called them. Blind watchmen… loving to sleep…leading the flock astray.   (Author's Note: Oh Notre Dame, listen, we used to think you were something special, but you are led by false Shepherds.)

Not all of the churches

If you are a pastor and have read this far then I am probably not talking about you. I have met a few courageous men who boldly live out the command to "lead them out." You know who you are. You are the one's who have been criticized, belittled, and called names by the "pimp in the pulpit" at the big church downtown.

You see, to him, the church is a business…an enterprise…a social club totally dependant on butts and bucks. It is a place to make business contacts, network with others in the community, and soothe one's conscience through weekly attendance and philanthropy. It is no different from a whore house where a woman's body is sold for the pleasure of another. Love-less intercourse is prostitution. Most church goers love the service that Jesus provides (membership has its privileges) but don't really know the Jesus who provides it.

I'll be honest. I've been afraid to say some of these things for fear of alienating even more pastors. I was afraid that my harshness might alienate those "frozen chosen" pastors and eliminate opportunities to "minister" to their congregations. That's where I have pimped-out my call. The pastors are not the answer, they are the problem. (Author's note, this shoe fits Notre Dame)

Instead of cleaning out Congress perhaps we should start by cleaning out the pulpit. Judgment begins first in the house of God. America is a reflection of the churches and the churches are a reflection of the pulpits. It is time to "throw the bums out"…even if they do hide behind the "touch not my anointed." When a football team is under-performing who gets the boot? Yep, the coach.

Allow me to be frank as I cut to the chase. Pick up your family and get out of the mausoleum you are attending and find a place that serves the Lord. I couldn't care less how many generations your family has been a member, how many pews your family has donated, and how many of your friends attend. Sitting in a pew every Sunday is not serving the Lord, it is the Lord serving you. The feel-good Gospel is a fraud. Jesus taught self-sacrifice not self-fulfillment. *"Greater love has no man than this than he would lay down his life for his friends…."* Love demands sacrifice. What have you sacrificed for your faith? You are engaging in Spiritual welfare…living off of the efforts of others.

Start fighting back by no longer giving them your money. Don't allow them to hit you over the head with the "bring all of the tithes into the storehouse" hammer without asking yourself some very important questions. What is a storehouse and what is its purpose? What does the Scripture mean by "meat in my house" and who is the meat for? Are there families in your "church" who are losing their homes? Is that not who the "meat in the house" was stored up for or were the storehouse funds used for a new parking lot?

Is the purpose of the tithe (by the way, my wife and I believe in tithing) to pay senior pastors, associate pastors, youth ministers, worship leaders, and secretaries to do "ministry?" Can't you "tithe" different places? Did the New Testament church teach the concept of "professional" Christians or were the elders of the church also tent-makers? Does "meat in my house" mean bigger buildings, paved parking lots, and padded pews? Is your "church" experiencing a budget crunch right now because they have eaten the meat that should have been placed in the storehouse? I know, "let them eat blacktop."

Is storehouse money supposed to be spent on the already converted or on seeking and saving that which is lost? What percent of your church's budget go to "missions"…as if that is a separate job…in comparison to utilities, paper, salaries, and operating expenses?

Don't stop giving, just change where you give. Find a ministry that is using the money to reach out to the community and send your tithe there. Remember, it is the "Lord's house" into which your finances are to be offered….not some social club to which your tithe is nothing more than monthly dues. It is time you asked yourself if the Spirit still dwells in your church.

My wife and I have spent the last few weeks reading the book of Acts in our morning devotionals. You should do the same. They spread the Gospel around the world at great personal peril and sacrifice. The self-serving American-Church is a pathetic step-child to Christianity's founding fathers.

Most churches love money, chase money, compromise over money. A pastor in New York was just fired from his $600,000 salary! The national average for pastors is $84,426! No wonder they won't speak against sin! Why not include those wealthy homosexuals in the congregation!

People have asked me to start a church. I tell them that they are nuts. Truth empties churches, it doesn't fill them. My friend Flip Benham says guys like me would be the Dr. Kervorkian of church growth. What man of God would want to wipe noses when he could fight evil? No thanks. At least on the streets I can recognize the enemy.

"And as they departed, Jesus began to say unto the multitudes concerning John, What went ye out into the wilderness to see? A reed shaken with the wind? But what went ye out for to see? A man clothed in soft raiment? Behold, they that wear soft clothing are in kings' houses." Yep, the pimps are the ones wearing the nice clothes. Funny isn't it? The pimps in the pulpits accuse street preachers of being undignified. Thank you Coach Dave for your insights from the Holy Spirit.

"And you took your sons and daughters whom you bore to me and sacrificed them as food to the idols. Was your prostitution not enough? You slaughtered my children and sacrificed them to the idols. In all your detestable practices and your prostitution you did not remember the days of your youth, when you were naked and bare, kicking about in your blood. Woe! Woe to you, declares the Sovereign LORD. In addition to all your other wickedness, you built a mound for yourself and made a lofty shrine in every public square" (*Ezekiel 16:20-24*).

This must indeed tie to Notre Dame, although it is so much bigger than Notre Dame, yet since one would look upon them as the flagship of Christian Universities, especially Catholic, their evil must be exposed. Catholic and other Christian schools and universities have been infected by the world. Get on your knees and pray for those running such institutions and those entering. Get on your knees and cry out, listen to the Lord and do it now! Souls are perishing, do it now! Pray for them, and know that the Shepherds can do what they should do if we cover them in prayer, please do it now! In Ephesians it says, "This I say therefore, and testify in the Lord, that ye henceforth walk not as other Gentiles walk, in the vanity of their mind, Having the understanding darkened, being alienated from the life of God through the ignorance that is in them, because of the blindness of their heart: Who being past feeling have given themselves over to lasciviousness, to work all uncleanness with greediness.

But ye have not so learned Christ; If indeed ye have heard him, and have been taught by him, as the truth is in Jesus: That ye put off concerning the former manner of life the old man, which is corrupt according to the deceitful lusts: And be renewed in the Spirit of your mind; And that ye put on the new man, which after God is created in righteousness and true holiness. Wherefore putting away lying, speak every man truth with his neighbor: for we are members one of another. Be ye angry, and sin not: let not the sun go down upon your wrath: Neither give place to the devil. Let him that stole steal no more: but rather let him labor, working with [his] hands the thing which is good, that he may have to give to him that needs.

Let no corrupt communication proceed out of your mouth, but that which is good to the use of edifying, that it may minister grace to the hearers. And grieve not the holy Spirit of God, whereby ye are sealed to the day of redemption. Let all bitterness, and wrath, and anger, and clamor, and evil-speaking, be put away from you, with all malice: And be ye kind one to another, tender-hearted, forgiving one another, even as God for Christ's sake hath forgiven you.

Be ye therefore followers of God, as dear children; And walk in love, as Christ also has loved us, and has given himself for us an offering and a sacrifice to God for a sweet-smelling savor. But lewdness and all uncleanness or covetousness, let it not be once named among you, as becomes saints; Neither filthiness, nor foolish talking, nor jesting, which are not convenient: but rather giving of thanks. For this you know, that no lewd, nor unclean person, nor covetous man, who is an idolater, has any inheritance in the kingdom of Christ and of God.

Let no man deceive you with vain words: for because of these things comes the wrath of God upon the children of disobedience. Be ye not therefore partakers with them.

For you were sometime darkness, but now are you light in the Lord: walk as children of light; (For the fruit of the Spirit is in all goodness, and righteousness, and truth.)

Proving what is acceptable to the Lord. And have no fellowship with the unfruitful works of darkness, but rather reprove them (Authors note: like those shining light on Notre Dame). For it is a shame even to speak of those things which are done by them in secret. But all things that are reproved are made manifest by the light: for whatever does make manifest is light. Wherefore he says, Awake, you that sleep, and arise from the dead, and Christ will give you light. See then that ye walk circumspectly, not as fools, but as wise, redeeming the time, because the days are evil.

Hopefully Fr. Tyson, Fr. Jenkins, and other Shepherds will see the light of Christ in the words of Dr. Keyes, so that they are no longer seen as fools, but become wise, accepting loving chastisement for their evil.

As you read this wise counsel to Shepherds, you will hear and see Truth. This does not go forth only to those responsible for the evils at Notre Dame, but to the Shepherds around the world, in all their different roles, as leaders, teachers, decision makers that affect the lives and souls of others. Pray that the Holy Spirit will open your eyes and ears.

3

LETTER TO FR. DAVID TYSON, SUPERIOR TO FR. JENKINS

FROM DR. ALAN KEYES

…no man is with us, see, God is witness betwixt me and thee (Genesis 31:50).

But Peter and John answered and said unto them, whether it be right in the sight of God to hearken unto you more than unto God, judge ye (Acts 4:19).

Then said Paul unto him, God shall smite thee, thou whited wall: for sittest thou to judge me after the law, and commandest me to be smitten contrary to the law (Acts 23:3)?

Dare any of you, having a matter against another, go to law before the unjust, and not before the saints? Do ye not know that the saints shall judge the world? And if the world shall be judged by you, are ye unworthy to judge the smallest matters? Know ye not that we shall judge angels? How much more things that pertain to this life? If then ye have judgments of things pertaining to this life, do you set them to judge who are least esteemed in the church? I speak to your shame (1Corinthians 6:1-4).

An obstacle set in the way, so that one is likely to fall over it, is called scandalum, a stumbling-block. So in the course of the spiritual way one is exposed to a spiritual fall by the deed or act of another, who by his advice or persuasion or example draws you to commit sin; and this is properly called scandal (Thomas Aquinas, Of Scandal).

To the Reverend Father David Tyson
Provincial of the Indiana Province
The Congregation of Holy Cross

Dear Sir,
SUMMARY
We are writing to seek redress of grievances we have suffered at the hands of Father John Jenkins, a member of your order. We approach you in the first instance because of your special responsibility for the spiritual welfare of members of your order who are part of the University of Notre Dame community. We must in good conscience inform you that, by abuse of his authority as President of the University of Notre Dame:

1) He has scandalized us and other members of the community of the faithful by his role in the decision taken by the University of Notre Dame, in defiance of the explicit direction of Church leaders, to extend a scandalous commencement speaking invitation and honorary degree to Barack Obama, who has become the focus of abortion evil in the world today;

2) To cover this scandalous decision, he ordered the University Police to prevent us from fulfilling our obligation, under God's law and the Church's teaching, to witness to truth so that young souls affected by his scandalous action would not be lost through obstinate commitment to the sins it encourages;

3) Aside from the obstacle it posed to the fulfillment of our moral obligation toward endangered souls, his action appears to give moral license to similar steps by civil authorities to discourage pro-life witness, thus extending the scandalous demoralization it involves to the whole pro-life movement;

4) The posture of indifference to evil and contempt for right action exemplified by his behavior promotes culpable moral apathy in the community of the faithful, encouraging in Catholics and others the lukewarm disposi-

tion which the Scripture tells us is most emphatically rejected by Christ.

To address these grievances, we respectfully request that you:

1) Immediately grant us a hearing so that we may formally detail the moral and material harm we have suffered at the hands of a member of your order;

2) Request and require that Father Jenkins, and any others of your order who may be involved with him in this matter, appear at the said hearing to respond to our charges against him;

3) Render judgment and immediate relief from the harm done to us, and others of the community of the faithful acting as we do, including but not limited to the immediate, public and complete withdrawal of all charges brought against us by the University before the civil authorities and the immediate cessation of all acts that persecute individuals witnessing to truth in accordance with divine law and the teachings and direction of the Church;

4) In lieu of a public apology, and In light of the urgent need to repair this ongoing scandal and prevent further scandals like it, we ask that you join us in appealing to the appropriate Church authorities, including the Bishop of the Diocese in which Notre Dame is located, for a proper investigation of these events, and the imposition of such just penalties as it may warrant upon all those members of the Catholic community responsible for this publicly scandalous injury to good morals;

5) In light of the injury to good morals inflicted by the invitation to Barack Obama, in which Father Jenkins played a major part, we ask that you join us in demanding an immediate end to the ongoing scandal it occasions, which has already produced victims, but which is likely to produce many millions more. As long as Notre Dame's invitation and offer of an honorary degree are extended, the scandalous wrong continues.

Narrative and Explanation

On Friday May 8, 2009 we were detained by the civil authorities at the behest of Father Jenkins and others authorized for the time being to act for the University of Notre Dame. At the time we were engaged in prayerful and peaceful witness to truth against the invitation extended by Father Jenkins et al to Barack Obama to be the university's commencement speaker and to receive an honorary degree.

The said invitation contravenes the Church's directive to the Catholic community to extend no such honors to those who "act in defiance of our fundamental moral principles." By this public show of defiance, Father Jenkins et al severely injure good morals. As Bishop D'Arcy said in his statement to the faithful "the outpouring of hundreds of thousands who are shocked by the invitation clearly demonstrates, that this invitation has, in fact, scandalized many Catholics and other people of goodwill.

In my office alone, there have been over 3,300 messages of shock, dismay and outrage, and they are still coming in. It seems that the action in itself speaks so loudly that people have not been able to hear the words of Father Jenkins, and indeed, the action has suggested approval to many."

Bishop D'Arcy's statement makes clear that per se the scandal has already injured thousands, if not hundreds of thousands of people. Archbishop Raymond Burke, Prefect of the Supreme Tribunal of the Apostolic Signatura, in a speech at the National Catholic Prayer Breakfast in Washington, DC stated emphatically that "The profound granting of an honorary doctorate at Notre Dame University to our President who is aggressively advancing an anti-life and anti-family agenda is a source of the gravest scandal."

Since the invitation involves Barack Obama, the moral injury caused by the scandal will reach throughout the world, where many millions who cannot and will not be exposed to any extenuating explanation will be exposed to the scandal it inherently occasions. Moreover, the extenuating effect of any explanations of the invitation must be judged in light of the fact that students at the University of Notre Dame have been exposed to Father Jenkins' influence for years, yet press reports indicate that a large majority of them support and admire a leader whose views and actions aggressively promote what the Church declares to be objectively wrong and sinful. Father Jenkins et al appear to have been gravely derelict in their responsibility for the souls entrusted to their educational care.

Their invitation can only aggravate the damage produced by this dereliction by appearing to honor the disordered choice resulting from it. According to Church law their scandalous conduct calls for investigation by appropriate authorities and the imposition of a just penalty.

Now in defense of their scandalous wrong action, Father Jenkins et al have perpetrated new scandal by directly impeding the just and righteous efforts of those who seek to correct the scandalous impression created their faulty decision. Through the writings and teaching of the Holy Father and other Church authorities the faithful have been enjoined to pray, speak and act to achieve an end to the heinous practice of abortion, and the unjust judgments and laws that purport to legitimize it.

In his aforementioned speech at the National Catholic Prayer Breakfast Archbishop Burke stressed that "our encounter with the world must be clear and uncompromising."

In accordance with this injunction, and in a manner strictly respectful of the requirements of prayerful love, decency and civil order, we stepped onto the grounds of the UND campus. Mindful of the University's special claim to the patronage of Our Lady, we were praying the rosary and pushing before us strollers representing the words of Christ, to wit, that offenses such as abortion committed against children are in fact done to Christ himself. What we did strictly accords with the obligations of right action, both as regards the teaching of the Church, the words of Christ and the law of God.

Whereas the decision by Father Jenkins et al gave the scandalous impression that those who are part of the community of faith regard the slaughter of innocent children as a matter of such indifference that it is possible to applaud and honor the apparent success of those who advocate and directly support it;

And whereas media reports and our own direct experience suggested that students at the University of Notre Dame have accepted and obstinately acted upon this view; And whereas by their conduct they showed contempt and disapproval for those who followed the law of God and the teaching of the church in respect of this view, indicating a firm, obstinate and contumacious commitment to wrongdoing;

We sought to provide clear and present witness to members of the Notre Dame community of the error that endangered their salvation in accordance with the true spirit and aim of charitable love, which is concerned above all with the spiritual salvation of every soul, not solely or even mainly with the strength and comfort of the body. We acted rightly and in accordance with true charity, and so, by God and the Church's teaching, we had the right to act as we did.

In direct contravention of this right, Father Jenkins, et al issued an order to ban us from the UND campus. This order literally put a stumbling block in the path of our fulfillment of our duty as determined by God's law and the Church's teaching. It sought forcibly to persuade us to ignore spiritual danger to our fellow believers and thus by omission to sin against justice and charity. It is therefore an occasion of sin and an unlawful act in terms of the law that governs the community of the faithful. (If we knew, for example that, with the collusion of the University administration, members of the Notre Dame community were being covertly done to death, and we sought to enter the campus to warn them of the danger, who would fail to recognize that we acted rightly in doing so? Who would fail to recognize the crime committed by members of the university administration who abused their authority in order to impel civil authorities to prevent the warning we sought to give? What it is right to do when only physical danger is involved, it is, in the eyes of God and the Church even more imperatively right to do when seeking to remedy mortal danger to the soul.)

So despite the unlawful order issued by Father Jenkins et al, we continued with our prayerful witness to truth. By their command, the university police arrested us and turned us over to the civil authorities for judgment and punishment. The action order by Father Jenkins, et al may or may not have been in accordance with their legal rights under the civil laws of property, since property rights are in certain circumstances constrained and conditioned by respect for civil rights such as the freedom of speech. As a matter of civil law that would be for the civil courts to determine. However, in the first instance (as a matter of spiritual concern dealing with events on the University's grounds, and thus subject first of all to the laws of God and the authority of the Church) their invocation of their property rights is subject to a higher law and a different authority. It involves a private judgment with respect to property they care for as a spiritual trust from the community of the faithful, who over the generations built and developed the University of Notre Dame in order to provide higher education that respects the truth exemplified in Jesus Christ and preserved through the centuries by the faithful activity of the Church community.

Notre Dame, and indeed all universities that claim to be part of the community of the faithful, do not exist solely as material buildings and land, etc. They are as well the sum total of the accrued results of past action, ongoing activity and preserved potential for the future, all contributing to the goal of education that respects the truth of Christ, in light of the teachings of the Church.

In its public mission statement the University of Notre Dame professes to be part of the community of the faithful. "God's way to us comes as communion, through the communities in which men and women live. This community includes the many theological traditions, liturgies, and spiritualities that fashion the life of the Church. A Catholic university draws its basic inspiration from Jesus Christ as the source of wisdom and from the conviction that in him all things can be brought to their completion. As a Catholic university, Notre Dame wishes to contribute to this educational mission."

Given its professed mission the University of Notre Dame has a responsibility to the Church, to the faithful and to the faith itself. Rightly understood, in fact, the University is not the property of any human persons, but a shared spiritual obligation to God, who has entrusted its fulfillment to particular persons as they promise faithfully to respect His will. Operating under the name and invoking the patronage of Our Lady, the Blessed Mother of God, the University has a further special spiritual obligation to act with particular regard for her unique contribution to the saving mission of the Body of Christ.

Some people have willfully misrepresented our prayerful witness as an instance of civil disobedience. We say that, to the contrary, it was an act of pious obedience. The command directly involved did not come from any civil authority, but from Father Jenkins, et al. When received by me and others, we were standing on University ground. As members of the community of faith both we and Father Jenkins et al are everywhere and always subject to the authority of the Church and the law of God. As our witness involved action strictly in accordance with the obligations and standards of right established by both, the order to interfere with it was, by the terms and standards of the law applicable to our behavior as members of the community of the faithful, an unlawful interference with our right action.

On our part, therefore, no disobedience to law was in any way intended or involved. Rather we obeyed the law of God and the directives of the church, while Father Jenkins et al abused their authority, using the civil authorities to cover their own malfeasance with respect to the spiritual welfare of the Notre Dame community. By thus unjustly commanding the UND police to detain us, and turn us over to the civil authorities for judgment, Father Jenkins, et al compounded the harm already done to the body of the faithful by their willful disregard for the Church's directive against honoring those who practice, advocate or otherwise support abortion. They exposed us to actions and penalties that may materially damage both our livelihood and reputations.

Their actions gave rise to the false imputation that we behaved unlawfully, despite their presumed knowledge that our action was in strict accordance with the standards of right that govern the community of the faithful. In this they bore false witness against us, in contravention of another of God's universally recognized commandments "you shall not bear false witness against your neighbor." By this false witness they expose the faithful to further scandal by bringing contempt and disrepute upon people of faith acting for aims and in a manner that strictly accord with right as judged by the standards of our community of faith.

We were shocked and grieved that those who profess to be our brothers and sisters in faith would authorize the civil authorities to persecute us for actions they know to be in strict accordance with our obligation to God and the Church. Catholics and other pro-life Christians have practiced prayerful, peaceful witness for truth through the whole tragic era of supposedly legalized abortion in the United States and elsewhere.

Beyond the harm done directly to those involved in this episode, the example of Notre Dame's harsh treatment of our witness appears to give moral license to the employment of similarly harsh methods by the civil authorities, even where they have until now respected the prayerful and peaceful nature of the activity as a legitimate exercise of the civil right of free speech.

An increase in such harsh actions could frighten and discourage members of the community of the faithful who might otherwise pursue righteous witness against evil. Thus, in order to defend their scandalous invitation to Barack Obama, Father Jenkins et al do further scandalous harm to the whole pro-life community and its mission to fulfill the moral obligation clearly imposed by Church teaching.

Requested Redress of Grievances

In light of these events it is clear that we, and any who acted as we did before or after the events in which we were involved, are the direct and public victims of an ongoing and grave public scandal directly perpetrated by Father Jenkins, et al. As Father Jenkins immediate superior in the Congregation of Holy Cross order, we appeal to you to for relief from this gravely scandalous behavior. We respectfully and urgently request that you:

1) Immediately grant us a hearing so that we may formally detail the moral and material harm we have suffered at the hands of a member of your order;

2) Request and require that Father Jenkins, and any others of your order who may be involved with him in this matter, appear at the said hearing to respond to our charges against him;

3) Render judgment and immediate relief from the harm done to us, and others of the community of the faithful acting as we do, including but not limited to the immediate, public and complete withdrawal of all charges brought against us by the University before the civil authorities and the immediate cessation of all acts that persecute individuals witnessing to truth in accordance with divine law and the teachings and direction of the Church;

4) In light of the urgent need to repair this ongoing scandal and prevent further scandals like it, we ask that you join us in appealing to the appropriate Church authorities, including the Bishop of the Diocese in which Notre Dame is located, for a proper investigation of these events, and the imposition of such just penalties as it may warrant upon all those members of the Catholic community responsible for this publicly scandalous injury of good morals;

5) In light of the injury to good morals inflicted by the invitation to Barack Obama, in which Father Jenkins played a major part, we ask that you join us in demanding an immediate end to the ongoing scandal it occasions, which has already produced victims, but which is likely to produce many millions more. As long as Notre Dame's invitation and offer of an honorary degree are extended, the scandalous wrong continues.

Conclusion

Because their actions take place in the context of a proposed event that necessarily focuses the attention of the world upon them, the scandal involved in the actions of Father Jenkins et al is an occasion of scandal to members of the community of the faithful throughout the world. This means that you, Bishop D'Arcy and other responsible Church authorities in America must act on behalf of those throughout the world whose responsibilities may be adversely affected by the ongoing scandal, including of course both the Head of your Order and the Holy Father in Rome.

As directly injured victims of the scandal, we will certainly be grateful for your performance of this duty, but we are sure responsible shepherds of the

Church throughout the world will pray to the Lord in thanksgiving for your diligence.

As members of the laity with no expertise in matters of canon law and procedure, we beg your indulgence and charitable aid if anything in this letter, or the manner of its presentation, fails to accord with forms that could only be known to such experts. However, for many centuries those such as you, who are charged with responsibility for overseeing the conduct of orders such as the Congregation of Holy Cross, have been asked to hear and judge cases that arise from the relations between their members and the larger community of the faithful in which they operate.

The laity has always relied upon the guidance, fairness, charity and justice before God of those charged with such responsibilities, before and in preference to any recourse to civil authorities who may operate without regard for the laws of God and the teachings of the Church.

In recent years, unfortunate and spiritually tragic events have in some measure damaged the laity's trust in these procedures. Such demoralization is precisely the sort of harm scandal involves. We trust however in your goodwill. As victims of the grave and spreading scandal now in progress we look forward to a prompt reply consistent with the urgent obligation to curtail the damage it does to us and to the community of the faithful throughout the world.

With Trust and Respect,

Alan L. Keyes

And Other Injured Parties, including: (Author's note: Many other saints joined us later.)

Daniel LaFree
Mishawaka, IN
Karen Mack
South Bend, IN
Karol Pasierbowicz
South Bend, IN
Mary Claire Chabot
Walkerton, IN
Bob Bramer
South Bend, IN
Missy Smith

Washington D.C.
Andrew Beacham
Elkhart, IN
Dr. Gregory Thompson
Humansville, MO
Gale Dodd
Granger, IN
Joyce Dodd
Granger, IN
Patrick Flynn
Pickney, MI
William Kee
Grand Prairie, TX
Jeanne Kee
Grand Prairie, TX
Steve Tucker
Milford, IN
Jane Brennan
Centennial, CO
Laura Rholing
Denver, CO
Ed Schaub
Buckhorn, NM
David Templeton
Huntington, IN
Tom Chanteloup
Cincinnati, OH
Ron Brock
San Diego, CA
Randall Terry
Falls Church, VA
Tui Bombeck
Washington, D.C.
Cindy Vorhees
South Bend, IN

STATE OF INDIANA) IN THE ST. JOSEPH SUPERIOR COURT
) SS:
ST. JOSEPH COUNTY)
)
STATE OF INDIANA)
)
VS.

Defendant	Case No.
JOHN AMES	71D01-0905-CM-03639
DEBORAH ANDERSON	71D01-0905-CM-03710
ANDREW BEACHAM	71D01-0905-CM-03389
JOAN BELL	71D01-0905-CM-03657
TAMIAS BEN-MAGDID	71D01-0905-CM-03667
ELEANORBRADY	71D01-0905-CM-03690
DR. ROBERT BRAMER	71D01-0905-CM-03387
JANE BRENNAN	71D01-0905-CM-03404
RONALD BROCK	71D01-0905-CM-03401
RONALD BROCK	71D01-0905-CM-03636
EDMUND BROPHY	71D01-0905-CM-03687
ROBERT BUCHTA	71D01-0905-CM-03699
MARYCHABOT	71D01-0905-CM-03392
THOMAS CHANTELOUP	71D01-0905-CM-03398
TRACEYCHASE	71D01-0905-CM-03706
JEAN CHASE	71D01-0905-CM-03709
MARYCOLSCH	71D01-0905-CM-03652
CAROLANN CYR	71D01-0905-CM-03621
ESTHER CYR	71D01-0905-CM-03626
HARRYDIMERTS	71D01-0905-CM-03705
EDWARD FADDOUL	71D01-0905-CM-03654
BRIGID FARANDA	71D01-0905-CM-03695
RONALD FINK	71D01-0905-CM-03685
PATRICK FLYNN	71D01-0905-CM-03405
JAMES FRITZ	71D01-0905-CM-03638
MARYGIROUX	71D01-0905-CM-03704
DENNISHATMAKER	71D01-0905-CM-03721
DR. CHARLES JACKSON	71D01-0905-CM-03693
GEORGE JOHNSON	71D01-0905-CM-03653

GEORGE JOHNSON 71D01-0905-CM-03707
WILLIAMKEE 71D01-0905-CM-03246
JEAN KEE 71D01-0905-CM-03386
DR. ALANKEYES 71D01-0905-CM-03391
DR. ALANKEYES 71D01-0905-CM-03619
BRIAN KINDZIA 71D01-0905-CM-03663
KATHLEENKUHNS 71D01-0905-CM-03686
MARYLAFRANCIS 71D01-0905-CM-03692
JOSEPH LANDRY 71D01-0905-CM-03666
PASTORJOSEPH LARSON 71D01-0905-CM-03663
SAMANTHALINNEMANN 71D01-0905-CM-03655
KURT LINNEMANN 71D01-0905-CM-03656
KAREN MACK 71D01-0905-CM-03395
KAREN MACK 71D01-0905-CM-03622
EDMUND MARINO 71D01-0905-CM-03715
ARNOLD MATHESON 71D01-0905-CM-03684
MICHAEL MCBRIDE 71D01-0905-CM-03698
NORMAMCCORVEY 71D01-0905-CM-03689
MARGARETMCKEE 71D01-0905-CM-03623
LUIS MENCHACA 71D01-0905-CM-03668
SISTER LOISMITORAJ 71D01-0905-CM-03714
DR.MONICAMILLER 71D01-0905-CM-03717
LUDOVIT MINJARIK................................. 71D01-0905-CM-03637
DAVID MITCHELL 71D01-0905-CM-03665
ANNE MITZEL 71D01-0905-CM-03720
ROBERT MORE 71D01-0905-CM-03723
MICHAEL O'CONNELL 71D01-0905-CM-03696
JOSEPH O'HARA 71D01-0905-CM-03661
JOSEPH O'HARA 71D01-0905-CM-03713
GEORGE OFFERMAN 71D01-0905-CM-03620
JUDITH PARRAN 71D01-0905-CM-03719
KAROL PASIERBOWICZ 71D01-0905-CM-03402
CHARLES PEARSALL 71D01-0905-CM-03627
PAUL PETKO 71D01-0905-CM-03630
RONALD PLATT 71D01-0905-CM-03697
DR. TERESERACHOR-BESTE 71D01-0905-CM-03722
MELVIN REDFORD 71D01-0905-CM-03634
ROBINREIERSON 71D01-0905-CM-03708

VICKIEREIERSON 71D01-0905-CM-03718
RICHARD RETTA 71D01-0905-CM-03639
LAURAROHLING 71D01-0905-CM-03390
RALPH ROHNER 71D01-0905-CM-03702
THOMAS ROOT 71D01-0905-CM-03662
LINDASCHMIDT 71D01-0905-CM-03716
MARJORIE SMITH 71D01-0905-CM-03403
MARJORIE SMITH 71D01-0905-CM-03624
JACK SMITH 71D01-0905-CM-03651
RITASPARROW 71D01-0905-CM-03688
DAVID TEMPLETON 71D01-0905-CM-03394
DAVID TEMPLETON 71D01-0905-CM-03631
LINDATERRY 71D01-0905-CM-03694
BRYAN TERRY 71D01-0905-CM-03700
DR. GREGORYTHOMPSON 71D01-0905-CM-03385
DR. GREGORYTHOMPSON 71D01-0905-CM-03632
BETH THORREZ 71D01-0905-CM-03659
JOETORNICHIO 71D01-0905-CM-03701
STEPHEN TUCKER 71D01-0905-CM-03399
CYNTHIAVOORHEES 71D01-0905-CM-03393
FATHER NORMAN WESLIN 71D01-0905-CM-03625
FATHER NORMAN WESLIN 71D01-0905-CM-03660
JACK WITUCKI 71D01-0905-CM-03650

Dr. Keyes, you have been given a gift by the Lord, may those that are in Leadership hear His voice speaking through your words. May the Shepherds of Notre Dame, all their leaders, stop listening to the secular world, especially as it speaks through attorneys that would have you listen to their wisdom, instead of God's wisdom.

Listen up Notre Dame Shepherds and all in the churches and ministries, Thus says the LORD: "I the LORD search the heart, I try the reins, even to give every man according to his ways, and according to the fruit of his doings." Know that I pray for your souls and that your stronghold of Pride will be broken so that you can hear the Word of the LORD. Right now, as you have put stumbling blocks in front of Christian brethren, which is an abomination to God. Those that speak the Truth of the Lord would have to give the following warning because of their actions, to all that would come into Notre Dame's presence saying, *"And then, if any man* (Fr. Jenkins, et al) *shall say to you, Lo, here is Christ; or lo, he is there; believe him not for false Christs, and false prophets will rise, and will show signs and wonders, to seduce, if it were possible, even the elect. But take ye heed: behold, I have foretold you all things"* (Mark 13:21-23).

Shepherds doing things their own way, each of your souls is at great risk, you who once sought the Truth of God, listen to those things that are an abomination to God:

"There are six things the LORD hates, seven that are detestable to him: haughty eyes, (Many Shepherds, including the leaders of Notre Dame and their superiors.) *a lying tongue,* (I ask, have I become your enemy for telling you the Truth?) *hands that shed innocent blood,* (Shepherds culpable, Notre Dame supporters of Obama.) *a heart that devises wicked schemes,* (Jesus sees your heart, Satan loves how you are.) *feet that are quick to rush into evil,* (Arrest those that speak for lives and souls of young.) *a false witness who pours out lies* (Call God true, and all men (Notre Dame) liars.) *and a man who stirs up dissension among brothers"* (Notre Dame et al, guilty) (Proverbs 6:16-19).

Are the Shepherds of the Christian schools and universities no more than Hirelings?

4

HIRED SHEPHERDS!

"I am the good shepherd: the good shepherd giveth his life for the sheep. But he that is an hireling, and not the shepherd, whose own the sheep are not, seeth the wolf coming, and leaveth the sheep, and fleeth: and the wolf catcheth them, and scattereth the sheep" (John 10:11).

I might as well ride this horse while I am on it. My commentary, Christian Pimps, blew the door of my email server off. I figured it would, but not in the way that it did.

The overwhelming response was heart-wrenching as I read story after story of the horror some folks have been put through by "local" churches (A. note: Shepherds). The refrain usually took one of two paths as writer's spelled out for me their stories. Some were tales of separation from life-long churches because they had the courage to question the status-quo by addressing the leadership (Shepherds) with many of the issues mentioned in Christian Pimps. Others were heart-sick over the un-Biblical practice of debt accumulation as the leadership ignored their cries and continued on with their "church growth" schemes as the integrity of the Word was diminished in the slide toward "relationship" evangelism.

To put it in medical terms, I hit a nerve. It is disheartening to hear from so many disaffected, disillusioned, wounded, no-longer church goers. Why have so many Christians dropped out of church? Rebellious sheep I suppose.....

But at the same time I was encouraged. There are millions of believers who are no longer part of the "church scene" who are passionately following hard after Jesus. Christianity operates best when we realize it is a relationship, not a religion. Many others share my hatred of "religion" and the box that it puts adherents in to. Where the Spirit of the Lord is there is Liberty! And many have found the freedom of worship outside the stained-glassed fortresses. (True Shepherds would repent and bring the sheep back to fellowship.)

Having said all of that, I recently promised to take on another issue, that of "the hirelings" in the pulpits.

Let me remind you that I am not a theologian; I have never attended seminary, and do not consider myself an expert on any Biblical issue. But I can read, and I can think. As I have taken time to do as the Bereans who "searched the scriptures daily, whether those things were so." I have found that many things I previously had been taught just simply did not line-up with Scripture. It was through my own study that I ran across something that up to now no one has been able to refute to me. Perhaps you can....I am not afraid of the Truth.

Early in my walk I heard a pastor use a Scripture that is often repeated. In fact, I used it on a number of occasions. It was only by happenstance as I was reading the Bible one day that something jumped out at me that flew in the face of everything I had believed. I don't want to shake your faith, or take away one of the church's catch phrases, but ever since I saw this truth I stopped misusing the verse. Buckle up...let's go for a short ride.

As I said, I am not a Bible teacher, but I can read. Here is the Scripture that I see so often misapplied. "*The thief cometh not, but for to steal, and to kill, and to destroy*" (John 10:10). Now for years I believed that the "the thief" mentioned here was the Devil. It is a pet verse of those who are "under attack" by the enemy. I do believe that the Devil is a thief, but allow me to propose to you that the Devil is not "the thief" that Jesus is warning about in this regularly quoted verse.

No my friends, the thief is not the Devil, but the "false shepherd," the same thief that I referred as "pimps." Please take a moment and read John 10:1:16.

In the very first verse Jesus identifies the thief for us. "*Verily, verily, I say unto you, He that entereth not by the door into the sheepfold, but climbeth up some other way, the same is a thief and a robber.*" Jesus tells us that the one who enters by the door is the shepherd (v.2) and that He (Jesus) is the door. (v.9). The one who enters any other way is a "thief and robber" (v.1) as clearly identified by Jesus.

He tells us that the sheep "hear his (true shepherd's) voice; he calls them by name, and he LEADS THEM OUT." (v. 3) The true shepherd "goes before the sheep" (v. 4) as he "leads them out."

But Jesus tells us in verse six that the folks to whom He was speaking "understood not," and He took more time to further explain. Beginning in verse seven He tells us that He was "the door" and that "all that came before him were thieves and robbers." (There it is again…He tells us who the thieves and robbers are…and it's not the devil.) The thieves are the false shepherds who will not lead the sheep to Jesus, "the door" (v. 9) through whom the sheep could be saved. (v.9). (Get ready…here it comes.)

In verse ten Jesus warns us that the previously identified thief (v.1 and v 7) has come to steal, kill, and destroy. The thief is not the Devil, but the false shepherd. (Still not convinced?)

Look who shows up in verse twelve…the wolf! Doesn't it make sense that the wolf is the Devil? We have two different characters here…the thief and the wolf.…the Devil can't be both. In fact, Jesus goes a step further to identify the thief for us by calling him a "hireling" and not the shepherd (v. 12). It is the "hireling" (false shepherd) who "seeth the wolf coming" (v. 12) and deserts his post. The hireling flees because he, "careth not for the sheep." (v. 13), but is only in it for his own personal gain. The thief (hireling) sees the wolf (Devil) coming, and flees. It is the hireling who has come to "kill, steal and destroy."

Some things never change. Those "hirelings" were the one's Jesus saved his greatest criticism for when He ran into them earlier, (only then He called them Pharisees) when He rebuked them because they *shut up the kingdom of heaven against men: for ye neither go in yourselves, neither suffer ye them that are entering to go in.*" (Remember, He also accused the hirelings of not being able to lead the sheep through the door). The Pharisees were the original hirelings. Read what Jesus said about them and ask yourself if they were any different from what stands in many of our pulpits today.

John 10 is clear if read with an open mind. Hirelings are Pharisees and the Pharisees were hirelings.…professional "ministers." Jesus warned us about both.

How can we possibly restore righteousness to this nation when we can't even get those who stand in the pulpit to honor the Word of God? How can we expect our elected officials to stand publicly against evil when the "men of the cloth" are too cowardly to do so?

Jesus' anger was not directed towards the secular government but towards those who changed his house of prayer into a "den of thieves." He cleaned the house and today we need to do the same.

Christians have lost all credibility with the world. For the most part the public image of Christian leaders is money grubbing, hypocritical, and Republican, a far cry from the Christ we claim to serve.

America is in dire need of a revival. It will never happen with the hirelings currently occupying our pulpits. It is at their feet that we must lay the killing, stealing, and destroying of the Christian heritage from this nation. It is time for a reformation.

Instead of all of this talk about "reclaiming America" perhaps we should refocus on reclaiming our faith. Has there ever been an institution with more pathetic leadership than we see today in American Christianity? Nothing is more debilitating to an army than cowardly leadership. (Author's note, if your Shepherd is a "good ole boy" likable, but a talker, instead of a walker addressing the weightier issues of the day, then go find a real MAN of God who leads the sheep in his care into the battles facing our posterity, and gives his life to protect their souls).

There has always been a true elite of God's leaders. They are the meek who inherit the earth (Mat. 5:5). They weep and pray in secret, and defy earth and hell in public. They tremble when faced with danger, but die in their tracks sooner than turn back. They are like a shepherd defending his sheep or a mother protecting her young. They sacrifice without grumbling, give without calculation, suffer without groaning. Their price is above riches. They are the salt of the earth. For the cause of the kingdom, we need more of them." Anonymous Do you know many shepherds like that?

Don't be discouraged. The Lord's Church is thriving and on the advance, but you will never recognize it if you are focusing on the group of people gathered in the building down the street. Most of those sheep belong to a hireling, a false shepherd, and not to the Lord.

It is the hireling, the false shepherd that has come to steal, and kill, and destroy.

Allow the Lord to be your Shepherd. He leads us out, we hear His voice, and He lays down His life for us.

As my friend Flip Benham says, *"Everyone wants to follow Jesus until they find out where He is going. He is going to a cross and he asks you to take up yours and follow Him."*

It is time we decided to follow Jesus and not some hired hand.

I pray that all Shepherds will hear HIS voice and come back to following Christ, instead of their own ways. Please stop and pray for your Shepherd.

"There is only one who is good" (Matthew 19:17).

Jesus says: *"Why do you ask me about what is good? There is only one who is good. If you wish to enter into life, keep the commandments"* (Matthew 19:17). In the versions of the Evangelists Mark and Luke the question is phrased in this way: *"Why do you call me good? No one is good but God alone"* (Mark 10:18; Luke 18:19).

Before answering the question, Jesus wishes the young man to have a clear idea of why he asked his question. The "Good Teacher" points out to him—and to all of us—that the answer to the question, "What good must I do to have eternal life?" can only be found by turning one's mind and heart to the "one" who is good: *"no one is good but God alone"* (Mark 10:18; Luke 18:19). Only God can answer the question about what is good, because HE is Good.

To ask about the good, in fact, ultimately means to turn towards God, the fullness of goodness. Jesus shows that the young man's question is really a religious question, and that the goodness that attracts and at the same time obliges man has its source in God, and indeed it is God Himself. God alone is worthy of being loved *"with all one's heart, and with all one's souls, and with all one's mind"* (Matthew 22:37). He is the source of man's happiness. Jesus brings the question about morally good action back to its religious foundations, to the acknowledgment of God, who alone is goodness, fullness of life, and the final end of human activity, and perfect happiness.

The Church, instructed by the Teacher's words, believes that man, made in the image of the Creator, redeemed by the Blood of Christ and made holy by the presence of the Holy Spirit, has as the ultimate purpose of his life to live *"for the praise of God's glory"* (Eph. 1:12), striving to make each of his actions reflect the splendor of that glory. *"Know, then, O beautiful soul, that you are the image of God"* writes Saint Ambrose. *"Know that you are the glory of God* (1Cor. 11:7).

For all Christians, for all Shepherds, by understanding that none of us are good as God defines good, it can only be found in HIM alone. Pray for those that feel they can define goodness in their own wisdom, which will be a lie to their being, if it is defined and acted upon outside of God's wisdom. Shepherds, pray and then act, for the praise of God's glory, the sheep are depending on you to teach HIS Truth.

5

THE SHEPHERDS ARE SLEEPING

"My people are destroyed for lack of knowledge: Because you have rejected knowledge, I will also reject you, that you shall be no priest to me: seeing you have forgotten the law of your god, I will also forget your children. As they were increased, so they sinned against me: therefore will I change their glory into shame. They eat up the sin of my people, and they set their heart on their iniquity. And there shall be, like people, like priest: and I will punish them for their ways, and reward them their doings. For they shall eat, and not have enough: they shall be guilty of lewdness, and shall not increase: because they have ceased to take heed to the Lord" (*Hosea 4:6-8*).

As I think about my experience in jail with David, I was blessed to hear his heart and desire to serve the Lord, which was sadly stepped on because of the Shepherds in charge of what was once a great campus serving the Lord, having at one time, Shepherds with wisdom doing things only after first praying to God for His direction. It is only natural that evil comes from Fr. Jenkins and those in positions of leadership at Notre Dame, leaven has been introduced by Satan, and they are blinded to the will of God. Notice how 2 Timothy speaks about Notre Dame in the following:

But mark this: There will be terrible times in the last days. People will be lovers of themselves (Notre Dame), *lovers of money* (Notre Dame), *boastful* (Notre Dame), *proud* (Notre Dame), *abusive* (Notre Dame), *disobedient to their parents, ungrateful* (Notre Dame), *unholy* (Notre Dame), *without love* (Notre Dame), *unforgiving* (Notre Dame), *slanderous* (Notre Dame), *without self-control* (Notre Dame), *brutal, not lovers of the good* (Notre Dame), *treacherous* (Notre Dame), *rash* (Notre Dame), *conceited* (Notre Dame), *lovers of pleasure rather than lovers of God* (Notre Dame)— *having a form of godliness but denying its power* (Notre Dame, Shepherds, leaders, and many faculty). Have nothing to do with them.

They (Notre Dame Shepherds and those who would have it so) are the kind who worm their way into homes and gain control over weak-willed women, who are loaded down with sins and are swayed by all kinds of evil desires, always learning but never able to acknowledge the truth. Just as Jannes and Jambres opposed Moses, so also these men oppose the truth—men of depraved minds, who, as far as the faith is concerned, are rejected. But they will not get very far because, as in the case of those men, their folly will be clear to everyone.

Paul's Charge to Timothy (also any true Christians at Notre Dame, and true Christian contributors)

You, however, know all about my teaching, my way of life, my purpose, faith, patience, love, endurance, persecutions, sufferings—what kinds of things happened to me in Antioch, Iconium and Lystra, the persecutions I endured. Yet the Lord rescued me from all of them. In fact, everyone who wants to live a godly life in Christ Jesus will be persecuted, while evil men and impostors will go from bad to worse, deceiving and being deceived. But as for you, continue in what you have learned and have become convinced of, because you know those from whom you learned it, and how from infancy you have known the holy Scriptures, which are able to make you wise for salvation through faith in Christ Jesus. All Scripture is God-breathed and is useful for teaching, rebuking, correcting and training in righteousness, so that the man of God may be thoroughly equipped for every good work.

2 Timothy 4, Paul goes on with this exhortation:

In the presence of God and of Christ Jesus, who will judge the living and the dead, and in view of his appearing and his kingdom, I give you this charge (listen up Notre Dame Shepherds and return to Christ): Preach the Word; be prepared in season and out of season; correct, rebuke and encourage—with great patience and careful instruction. For the time will come when men (Notre Dame is proof) will not put up with sound doctrine. Instead, to suit their own desires, they will gather around them a great number of teachers to say what their itching ears want to hear. They will turn their ears away from the truth and turn aside to myths. But you, keep your head in all situations, endure hardship, do the work of an evangelist, discharge all the duties of your ministry.

Satan is hoping that Notre Dame and other Christian schools and colleges, will stay sleeping and blind, leading with their own wisdom, rather than God's wisdom. Leaven has been introduced into all the Christian schools, as they allow the world to change them. Please call me if you would like to reason with me and pray, call 417-894-5768.

The Shepherds are sleeping as they allow the wolves to come in to scatter and devour the sheep. Priests, pastors, ministry leaders, and church leaders, please do not call yourself a Christian, please do not take the name of Christ, in fact, please change your name, or change your conduct, if you are not personally leading Christians against the enemy, and trying to protect your neighbor with more than talk.

It seems obvious that you don't love the sheep in your care, you don't love your neighbor, and you don't love God, or you would do what HE says. You would give the impression that you care, since you give the impression with the words from your mouth, maybe we can just give you our money, invite our friends to give you money, and then, well just maybe we can build a bigger building, that can hold more of our friends to give you more money. Now how many babies did you keep from being murdered with your mouth? How many times did you personally try to stop the murder of a baby? How many souls did you let go to hell in the government education system? How many little girls and boys were molested in mind and body because you were silent while they went into the belly of the beast called government education.

I had someone write me and tell me that I should not say that pastors were going to put themselves at risk of hell for eternity if they did not tell the people in their congregation the truth about government schools and the need to get the children out. The letter was from some good friends of mine, and was meant for good. They felt that I was judging the heart and that only God could do that, and right they are about only God being able to judge the heart. But what I am required to judge by Scripture is the fruit or lack of it in my brothers and sisters in Christ. I am required to warn my brothers and sisters of anything that would put them at risk for eternity. My warning to get the children out of the atheistic and pagan government education system is to the sheep and the Shepherds. First, to tell the sheep to run from the government schools, that all have a cancer within, that they feed on the souls of the children, and that they are one of the greatest systems of child abuse known to man. I would then tell the sheep to run from a Shepherd that is not leading, and not warning about the issues affecting our families and nation. If the Shepherd is not warning, and helping the parents in every way possible, then get away from them, no matter how much pretty talk you hear. Pray for their souls, because they have indeed put themselves and others at risk.

Now, Shepherds, are you a hireling, or do you serve Christ. Do you cut and paste your Bible so that you are comfortable on your pillow. Have you denied yourself and picked up your cross? Have you died to yourself daily, as you ask your flock to do, or do you? Are you in action like Christ, or do you just talk a good story? You say that you love your neighbor and then let the murder of babies continue as you sit in your church telling jokes, or telling others something must be done, as you do nothing in the weightier matters of the day, hiding behind things like feeding the poor, clothing the naked, visiting the sick, etc. While these things should not be ignored, you are preparing your place with the goats, if you do not step up and lead as Christ would in the weightier issues of the day.

Where is your anguish as people are going to hell for eternity, did you judge that fornication is a sin that can send a church member to hell, did you judge that sodomy is a sin that can send a neighbor or friend to hell, did you judge that voting for anyone that supports murder or any sin puts them and others at risk of hell? What kind of Shepherd are you if you don't love your sheep to the point of wanting them in heaven for eternity.

In vain can we extenuate the matter, pastors, priests, and other supposedly Christian leaders can cry "peace, peace," but there is no peace. The war has actually begun. The next affronts that come from Washington D.C. will bring to Christians and this nation, bloodshed, corruption, moral decay, and more people at risk. Your brothers and sisters are already in the field. What is it that Christian leaders wish? What would you have? Is your life so dear and your peace so sweet that you are willing to purchase it with chains, slavery, and death for your neighbors? As Patrick Henry stated, "Forbid it Almighty God, I know not what course others may take, but as for me, give me liberty or give me death."

Shepherds, please remember to repent, and change your ways, so that you do not spend eternity out of the presence of God. Don't betray Jesus like Judas did, where Jesus would tell you that it would have been better if you had not been born.

- Have you done anything to stop the elderly health plan and other destructive plans and anti-Christian and anti-Constitution appointees being put forth by Obama?
- Have you done anything to put the leaders under the same plan they propose to put the people under in health care?
- Have you done anything to stop the communist anti Christ takeover of America?
- Would you allow unrepentant abortionists to be members of your church?
- Would you allow unrepentant pornography providers to be members of

your church?

- Would you allow those openly engaging in fornication to be members of your church?
- Would you allow those openly engaged in homosexuality to be members of your church?
- Would you allow any unrepentant sinner to be a member of your church and receive communion while in sin?
- Shepherd, pastor, priest, elder, what weightier matter are YOU taking on today?

Jesus would stand up to evil, Jesus would require repentance from sin, and would say to go and sin no more. Well, maybe you are nicer than Jesus, maybe you love people more than Jesus, maybe you are even smarter than Jesus, maybe you can tell people how good they are, and how to have their best life now, and fill your belly, and sleep at night as the sheep in your care go to hell. Well maybe Jesus will learn to be nice like you, let you disobey and sin, whatever you want to do, and will just let you go on into heaven, and maybe not, what do you think?

Fill in the blanks, "you are either with me or _____ __, you either gather with me, or you _____." "Why call me Lord, Lord, and then ___ __ what I say?" "The heart is _____ above all things?" "To know what to do and not do it is a ___."

6

MUST I TEAR AWAY THE LIMB THAT IS BOUND?

Then said Jesus to his disciples, *"If any man will come after me, let him deny himself, and take up his cross, and follow me. For whoever will save his life, shall lose it: and whoever will lose his life for my sake, shall find it. For what is a man profited, if he shall gain the whole world, and lose his own soul? Or what shall a man give in exchange for his soul?"* (Matthew 16:24-26).

When I was a boy there was a beautiful scarab that frequented the blackberry bushes in East Tennessee. The June bug was easily captured and, as my sisters picked berries, we boys tied threads from Momma's sewing box to a leg of the scarab and let it buzz around, tethered to our clutches. And, when it pulled from our clutches, thread still tied to its limb, it flew away, thinking it had broken those surly bonds. The branches of other bushes reached out and caught the strings and the June bug was entangled inescapably in something it could not understand or elude. Unless some tenderhearted human being recognized its plight, the June bug finally succumbed to its confinement, struggling to its last moment to tear away into freedom.

I wake every night from a nightmare that has me pulling at something that won't be broken by all my yearnings to be free. I try to reason my situation; nothing makes sense. What entangled me in this web?

My momma and daddy raised seven of us in the Appalachian Mountains back in the 40s and 50s. They were poor whites of Scots-Irish descent. They were God fearing and reverent of every bit of His creation. We learned a love of all life, in all of its forms. A baby from any mother born into this world was a miracle, as was this entire splendor called Life. A flower, a tree, a river, a dawn or sunset, all spectacles of this Eden, all life forms were God's creation and awesome and splendid.

Most of the time, our spiritual sustenance came from reflection but when we went to church we were Baptists. That was bout the only church around those hills.

All of my life, since my childhood, I have been awed by this creation and all its moments.

Nowadays, not understanding all of the world's mysteries, I would never presume to speak for God or imagine that I know what God thinks. Yet, it seems most probable that God would have wanted His creation to be good and that He would not want anything in His creation abused. I have to believe that God was pleased when Christianity became the guiding light for billions of people. Similarly, I cannot imagine that God would be pleased with any distortion, any usurping, any modification, any compromising of the conditions for His grace as given us in the Ten Commandments.

I believe that the Catholic Church has been one of the most stalwart defenders of all of the laws and principles of Christianity throughout its existence since Saints Peter and Paul. Even as a Protestant, I have always seen the Catholic Church as the strongest rock in Christianity; as the consistent purveyor of God's expectation of Man on earth. With the ever rising tide of capitulation to making allowances for almost any assault on Christianity, I have always believed that the Catholic Church would never yield.

Certainly, the one absolute, that Life is sacred and precious and shall not be sacrificed, and shall not be destroyed, has always been without a challenge in the Catholic Church. THOU SHALT NOT KILL. (Authors note: Even though there have been some bad Shepherds within the Catholic Church, just like other Christian churches, it is now necessary for the real Shepherds in the Catholic Church to start leading and standing in the gap, to take the next step in protecting lives and souls, to quit talking and start walking.)

It follows that the one steadfast extension of God's hand to protect the innocent little girl or little boy growing in the womb, would always be the firm guardianship of the Catholic Church. (Author's note: The Catholic Church has been great in standing, but is culpable in the slaughter of innocent life. Why? Because abortion will stop when the church says it stops, if the bishops would get out of their Cathedrals and be like Christ, and lead His sheep, the outcry would be so great it would stop the murder of babies. Where is the Bishop that follows in the shoes of Jesus, speaking HIS Truth, not allowing communion or membership in the church to any Catholic or Knight of Columbus that supports abortion, and starting with shunning any government leader that votes for or supports abortion in any way.)

In these terrible days, protection of the unborn baby, I believed, would never be compromised by the Catholic Church nor its many facilities.

As a society we have leaned on Catholic institutions to foster God's will, as we are given to understand that will. We have celebrated their wonderful furtherance of a moral and spiritual underpinning that only a perverted rationale could possible deny. Notre Dame du Lac has been such a stalwart. (Author's note: yet over the last 30 years it has taken a subtle but continuous journey into darkness, as leaven has been introduced and embraced more and more by the clergy, board, administration, and faculty. Even though in their blindness, you could never convince them that they are blind. They are riding the coat tails of prior generations when God was first in all parts of the education. Yet now HE takes a back seat to intellect, which has built a stronghold that does not allow their souls to see the light of wisdom as expressed by Christ and those that follow Him. As a result, Notre Dame has blood on her hands, which is an affront to Jesus, and His mother, whom they take the name of. I pray that all the donors are able to pray and see Christ in their hearts, and withhold any support to this worker of iniquity. It would be better for Notre Dame to burn to the ground than to be responsible for infecting the souls of more children and putting them at risk of hell for eternity. I would say that even the Bishop is ignorant, afraid, or willing to give a spirited rendition of the truth so as to keep the status quo, very un-Christ like.)

Now I am chosen to encourage Notre Dame's God-given destiny. I do not know, I cannot reason, the mysteries that converged to bring me to this surreal circumstance, a bond with faith that will not be broken lest I sever life or limb to be free.

I am in fear of imprisonment. My worldly body and mind cries that I may be bound into a cell of concrete and iron without supplication any day from the world outside the prison's wall. And, I agonize that I will not be physically, mentally, or spiritually able to endure the compound.

I try to orient the strands of circumstance that ended up tying me thusly and try to retread the path that brought me here. My reasoning breaks toward justifying my deserving of freedom. My thinking looks for words that might convince the potentates that I do not deserve imprisonment. Yet, I am torn immediately to see that my suffering is little, compared to the agony of a baby girl being torn to shreds by the forceps of an uncaring society. Does my pain approach that of a little boy being strangled to death in a poison salt solution, a brine of pain and suffering my feeble mind can only imagine?

I am so scared that the judge and the juries looking at my prayerful vigil at

Notre Dame will see only a pragmatic view toward justice for the Law. I am so scared that Notre Dame, its presidents, the prosecutor, the juries, will seek vengeance against my demonstration of faith instead of amelioration. I am so scared that I will find myself wasting away in a prison cell with a sentence that serves no person, no body, no institution, no society any good whatsoever.

And, finally, I am bound to think about the other gentle souls caught on the same tether, tied to a bond they may not escape. And, I pray to God; why would any entity prosecute and continue to persecute what basically amounts to a small band of old men and old women praying the Rosary and the Lord's prayer in a site that has all of God's glory as a preamble to its being.

I am, at once, ashamed that I cannot sleep for fear of my own day of reckoning and emboldened that God's will shall prevail, in spite of my fears and in spite of any institution's wayfaring from His intention.

David Tremble is a servant of the Lord standing in the Gap. He has experienced some of those in the Church, government, and education leadership, who are doing things by the wisdom of man, instead of God, and thus are spoken of in this passage: *"As a dog returns to its vomit, so a fool repeats his folly. Do you see a man wise in his own eyes? There is more hope for a fool than for him"* (Proverbs 26:11,12). Sadly these leaders at Notre Dame, are not living the Gospel that they may indeed try to slip into part of the academia, they are not living by example the words of Christ, where He says, *"and anyone who does not take his cross and follow me is not worthy of me. Whoever finds his life will lose it, and whoever loses his life for my sake will find it"* (Matthew 10: 38, 39).

May God open the eyes of these blind guides, and the Christians who support them because of blindness, and return them to Christ, and heal those that have been injured by their pride, disobedience, and silence, so that God will not speak as HE did in Zechariah 13:7 where he states, *"Awake, O sword, against my shepherd, against the man who is close to me!" declares the LORD Almighty. "Strike the shepherd, and the sheep will be scattered, and I will turn my hand against the little ones"* (Zechariah 13:7).

You have been warned about the yeast from the Shepherds at Notre Dame that has been implanted into many children's lives, and by the Grace of God, may you have understanding as the Apostles did in the Gospel. *"Then they understood that he was not telling them to guard against the yeast used in bread, but against the teaching of the Pharisees and Sadducees."* (Matt 16).

7

SHEEP WITHOUT SHEPHERDS

"...and upon this rock I will build my church; and the gates of hell shall not prevail against it" (Matthew 16:18).

There is no law in America any more. Now, don't take that the wrong way. There are plenty of LAWS in America, but there is no law. Lex Rex is an old legal term which, translated from the Latin, means simply "the Law is King." It is the premise upon which all natural law and our American Constitutional Republic was formed. No one is above the law and natural laws cannot be altered.

But recently in America we have seen this premise turned on its head. No longer *"Lex Rex, the law is king,"* but now *"Rex Lex the king is law"* is the prevailing system in our once-great republic. Our political leaders destroy the foundations of the nation by changing the laws to legalize the current most-popular sin.

"In those days there was no king in Israel: every man did that which was right in his own eyes." Jesus is no longer King over America. Without Him and His Precepts there is no law. Although we no longer live under a king we are far removed from the Republic that our Founders gave us. They rebelled over a tax on tea for heaven's sake!

But the thought of disobeying government is almost anathema to the Church Leadership today. Slowly but surely the chains of government are being forged for American Christianity and hardly a whimper from the "men of the cloth."

"Romans 13 commands us to obey the government, Coach" they tell me all of the time. *"Really?"* I ask. *"Why is it some of the great heroes of the Bible are those who refused to follow unrighteous leaders and unrighteous decrees?"* Have you considered Moses and Pharaoh, Daniel and King Darius, Shadrach, Meshach, Abednego and Nebuchadnezzar? Paul wrote two-thirds of the New Testament,

much of it from jail. Jesus himself rebelled by speaking the Truth against the government. It cost him His life.

When will the American Church leadership say, "Enough is Enough?"

I just recently returned from another "Shake The Nation" seminar in Idaho. We travel the country trying to awaken Christians to what is happening around us and our need to engage the culture. My friend, Tom Munds, spent three months organizing the event in Boise. He sent out fliers, visited churches, met pastors, advertised on radio and in print, using his own money. After the event the reaction was the same as everywhere we go.

"My goodness," the attendees say. *"Where are our pastors? Why aren't they telling us this stuff? We have to do something. There are more Christians than there are any other faiths."*

And what is it we are telling them when we hold a seminar?
- Abortion is Murder.
- Homosexuality and divorce are sin.
- Our schools have become Secular-Humanist factories.
- Our rights are God-given, not government-granted.
- God is King…..your government is not.
- Judgment begins in the house of God.
- It is our job to fight for Truth.
- American Christianity has lost His Salty Savor.
- Islam is a lie from the pit of hell.

The pastors never come. The sheep innately know something is terribly wrong but can't put a finger on the problem. We expose the Devil's game-plan and their eyes become opened, but they have no where to turn.

But the shepherds won't come. They are afraid of what they might hear. Christianity is an army without generals.

It reminds me of the monkeys….*hear no evil, see no evil, and speak no evil…* maybe if they just ignore it, it will all just go away. Well, the foundations of this nation are crumbling. We ignore it at our own peril. Can you say "California Supreme Court"?

"Those issues are political," our religious leaders say. *"Those issues are religious,"* our political leaders say, each lacking the courage to do what must be done.

You see, our pastors love to shepherd in the safety of the sheep-pen, but they have a Pilate's-basin approach to the land where the wolves roam. America needs her shepherds out in the streets. That is where the wolves are trolling, but the shepherds think commentating on the battle is the same as engaging in it. Howard Cosell spoke of the battle, Muhammad Ali engaged in it. Which one was known as "The Greatest?" Take it from me, when you stand-up and speak-up you better be prepared to duck. The enemy doesn't play fair -- they play to win. The IRS, media bombardment, character assassination, and lawsuits are just a few of the arrows sure to fly your way. Remember, opposition is the sign of progress. Shepherds are supposed to be brave enough to fight but we don't see them out much, so we know they're not guarding what has been given to them. They spend their time preparing sermons about sin, instead of leading an army to fight it.

So, I look at what is going on with the Judicial Tyranny in the State of California and across this nation, and I wonder when will "the church of Gulliver" arise? How long will righteousness continue to be tied down by the black-robed Lilliputians? Could it be that the Lord is allowing all of these things to come upon us to get His Body to stand up and fight?

Over the past eight years I have spent a lot of time defending the faith the best I know how. I have seen victory after victory slip from our hands because the "men of the cloth" were AWOL on the field of battle. I have traveled the land and personally witnessed:

- Judge Roy Moore' stand for the Ten Commandments only to be called a law-breaker and be abandoned by the shepherds when he was hauled off of the bench that he'd been elected to by the People.

- Terri Schiavo being murdered as the "shepherds" fed their flock in the safety of their sanctuaries. Instead of fighting for her life they encouraged folks to "get a living will."

- Women go into abortion mills as pastors drive by on their way to their Saturday morning tee-time. Sodomy legalized. Gambling legalized. Divorce legalized. Homo "marriage" legalized. All by judges who have no right to legislate and legislators who forget that they work "for the people."

- Homosexuality celebrated in government schools. A teacher ordered to remove a Bible from his desk. Christianity stripped from the schools of this nation while the pastors (Shepherds) support the un-Godly institution.
- Children snatched from their homes by "government social services."
- The pulpit silenced by the IRS in fear of losing their tax-exempt status.

So now the Lord brings another opponent our way. Government of the People, by the People, and for the People has been shredded by six Republican-appointed judges in California. The secular pastors are out in the streets praising the "wisdom" of the Court, while Christian pastors are safely secured in their sanctuaries where they curse the darkness of this day rather than being the light from which the evil must flee.

Allow me to repeat what I have said a thousand times. America's problems are not the politicians; her problems are in the pulpits. Let me prove a point.

Whenever you see a moral issue pop up in this land that is sanctioned by government should you "call your congressman" or your pastor? The correct answer is your pastor. He is supposed to speak for God.

That is why Jesus said the gates of hell will not prevail against THE CHURCH. There are certain battles mandated by Jesus that the Church must fight. Why should we expect our politicians to stand up for Truth when our pastors won't? If the pastors would speak, the politicians would begin to dance to a different drummer.

Gates don't move, they stand. The only way they prevail is if the Lord's Church doesn't storm them. Prayer is not enough, it requires action. Prayer is the power; it is the propulsion, the prevailing force through which the physical action is spiritualized.

"(*For the weapons of our warfare are not carnal, but mighty through God to the pulling down of strongholds.) Casting down imaginations, and every high thing that exalteth itself against the knowledge of God, and bringing into captivity every thought to the obedience of Christ; And having in a readiness to revenge all disobedience, when your obedience is fulfilled*" (2 Cor. 10:4-6).

The gates are the strongholds. Those occupying the gates do not honor God. Believers are called to pull them down, to storm the gates, to avenge all disobedience in our duty to honor God.

"*Unless I am convinced by proofs from Scriptures or by plain and clear reasons and arguments, I can and will not retract, for it is neither safe nor wise to do anything against conscience. Here I stand. I can do no other. God help me. Amen.*" Martin Luther 1521But our sheep have no shepherds. Rather than fighting the wolves they are hiding from them. "*I'll huff and I'll puff, and I'll blow the house down.*"

No wonder folks are worried about global warming. Prayer without action is nothing more than hot-air!

..and the Pulpits Are Silent

For among my people are found wicked men: they lay wait, as he that setteth snares; they set a trap, they catch men. As a cage is full of birds, so are their houses full of deceit: therefore they are become great, and waxen rich. They are waxen fat, they shine: yea, they overpass the deeds of the wicked: they judge not the cause, the cause of the fatherless, yet they prosper; and the right of the needy do they not judge. Shall I not visit for these things? saith the LORD: shall not my soul be avenged on such a nation as this (Jeremiah 5:26-31)?

Despite what the political parties would like you to believe, the problem in America is not the politicians, it is the pulpits. I hate to break the news to you, but most of America's pulpits are filled with cowardly men. They are a shame to the Christ they claim to serve.

Harsh words, aren't they? Not the type of thing that will make any friends in this "cheap-Grace" culture in which we live. But that's okay. I'm not looking to make friends.

I am about fed-up with what I see. How did we ever get such man-pleasing leaders? All that our fore-fathers held dear is being destroyed before our very eyes and hardly a peep from the pulpit. They don't want to hear it. It's the pulpiteers that I am talking about. They are concerned with being too harsh, they tell me that "Jesus is in control," that they are not "called" to fight evil and that "we should pray for our enemies."

Where have these guys come from? What we need is a return of the Voice of God thundering through the prophets standing in America's pulpits. Not the prissy Purpose Driven drivel passing as the Gospel today. The feminized-preachers of today cannot hold a candle to those who ushered in The Great Awakening which led to the American Revolution, and the abolition of slavery -- two world-changing events spearheaded by the pulpit.

Listen to the message of America's premiere preachers today. Rick Warren and his Purpose Driven Life have infiltrated the Church. Over 400,000 pastors have attended his conferences and over 40 million of his books have been sold. Wikipedia tells us *"Since September 2002, over 30,000 congregations, corporations, and sports teams across the United States have participated in a "40 Days of Purpose" emphasis. A May 2005 survey of American pastors and ministers conducted by George Barna asked Christian leaders to identify what books were the most influential on their lives and ministries."* The Purpose Driven Life was the most frequent response. Today's Christians are more familiar with the words of Warren than the Words of Jesus. Thousands of America's churches have used it in their Bible Studies and thousands of preachers preach Warren's message.

Joel Osteen was voted Most Influential Christian in 2006. His preaching style focuses on *"the goodness of God rather than sin."* He is a self-described *"Life-coach"* and *"thinks that there are probably others better qualified, or more gifted for explaining Bible verses. Osteen explains that he tries to teach Biblical principles in a simple way, emphasizing the power of love and a positive attitude."* Wikipedia. *"Presently, Osteen and several Lakewood Church team members travel across the nation, presenting programs in large stadiums to a paying public."* He has sold millions of books to millions of feel-good Christians.

While our nation is killing babies, our schools are indoctrinating Christian-kids in Secular Humanism, and "Truth has fallen in the streets," our preachers are attending church-growth seminars, using 'self-help" books to supplement the Bible, and chasing after the butts and bucks. They are fiddling while the nation burns, building their church rather than Christ's Kingdom.

- Public schools are destroying the faith of Christian children and the pulpits are silent.

- Legislation is introduced to remove the rights of parents and the pulpits are silent.

- Children are taught they came from apes and the pulpits are silent.

- Millions of children are "medicated" to control their behavior and the pulpits are silent.

- Gambling is promoted to pay for schools and the pulpit is silent.

- Precious babies are being murdered in the womb and the pulpits are silent.

- Planned Parenthood kills babies with our tax dollars and the pulpits are silent.

- Judges make laws and the pulpits are silent.

- Tolerance trumps Truth and the pulpits are silent.

- Sodomy is granted legal protection and the pulpits are silent.

- The institution of marriage is crumbling and the pulpits are silent.

- Obama says the Sermon on the Mount justifies gay marriage and the pulpits are silent.

- Government has replaced God as defender and provider and the pulpits are silent.

- Faith-based initiatives invite the government into the Church and the pulpits are silent.

- The IRS muzzles the voice of the Church and the pulpits are silent.

- Taxes are levied to do the work of the Church and the pulpits are silent.

- The Church locks arms with compassionate-conservatism and the pulpits are silent.

- Children's service agencies separate family members and the pulpits are silent.

- Self-help books replace the Bible and the pulpits are silent.

- *A Purpose Driven Life* is elevated above dying to self and the pulpits are silent.

- G.W. Bush says Christians and Muslims worship the same God and the pulpits are silent.

- The Constitution is ignored and the pulpits are silent.

- Pagans pray to open a session of Congress and the pulpits are silent.

- Our elected officials lie and steal and the pulpits are silent.

- Private property is stolen by government and the pulpits are silent.

- The earth is protected more than Father God is defended and the pulpits are silent.

- Illegal aliens over-run our borders and the pulpits are silent.

- The entertainment industry celebrates debauchery and the pulpits are silent.

From a bygone era, the sound from the pulpit rumbles throughout the ages. *Could a mariner sit idle if he heard the drowning cry? Could a doctor sit in comfort and just let his patients die? Could a fireman sit idle, let men burn and give no hand? Can you sit at ease in Zion with the world around you DAMNED?— Leonard Ravenhill*

Churches don't need new members half as much as they need the old bunch made over. There wouldn't be so many non-church goers if there were not so many non-going churches. Too many churches are little more than four walls and a roof.- Billy Sunday

The voice from the pulpit today sings a different song.

"The prophets prophesy falsely, and the priests bear rule by their means; and my people love to have it so: and what will ye do in the end thereof" (Jeremiah 5:31)?

Truth, justice and the American way are a thing of the past.

"None calleth for justice, nor any pleadeth for truth: they trust in vanity, and speak lies; they conceive mischief, and bring forth iniquity" (Isaiah 59:4). Tragically, the pulpits are silent.

God's word states, *"Do not be yoked together with unbelievers. For what do righteousness and wickedness have in common? Or what fellowship can light have with darkness? What harmony is there between Christ and Belial? What does a believer have in common with an unbeliever? What agreement is there between the temple of God and idols? For we are the temple of the living God. As God has said: "I will live with them and walk among them, and I will be their God, and they will be my people." "Therefore come out from them and be separate, says the Lord. Touch no unclean thing, and I will receive you. I will be a Father to you, and you will be my sons and daughters, says the Lord Almighty"(2 Cor. 6:14-18).*

8

CHURCH MILITANT AT NOTRE DAME

"Let your manner of life be without covetousness; and be content with such things as you have: for he has said, I will never leave you, nor forsake you. So that we may boldly say, The Lord is my helper, and I will not fear what man shall do to me. Remember them who have the rule over you, who have spoken to you the word of God: whose faith follow, considering the end of their manner of life. Jesus Christ the same yesterday, and to-day, and for ever. Be not carried about with divers and strange doctrines: for it is a good thing that the heart be established with grace; not with meats, which have not profited them that have been occupied in them (Hebrews 13:5-9).

Authors note: With Bishops and others church leaders of all Christian faiths safely hidden in their homes, a great opportunity to turn back evil was missed but by a few, a remnant that stood up to honor and glorify God. Whether you agree with Randal Terry or not, he was on the battle lines against the powers and principalities attacking through Notre Dame President Fr. Jenkins et al, and President Barack Obama et al. Keep your eyes focused on Christ, because it was not about Notre Dame, and it is not about Randal Terry. Yet Randal had his eyes fixed on Christ and innocent babies <u>while Notre Dame sinned and honored an unrepentant worker of iniquity, and allowed this evil to speak to the children and parents.</u>

Our Lady of Guadalupe conquered human sacrifice. Notre Dame now honors a man who promotes it.

by Randall Terry
Founder, Operation Rescue

<u>*Would Notre Dame invite Herod to speak—after he tried to kill Our Lady's Son, and slaughtered the Innocents in Bethlehem?*</u>

Who is Worse: Obama or Herod? You decide.
Herod authorized the slaughter of roughly 30 little boys in one small village

By contrast, in the 2 months since Obama took office, he has authorized the slaughter of thousands, and perhaps millions.
- Obama overturned the "Mexico City Policy," and ordered that your tax money pay for the murder of the innocent around the world. Forced abortion in China will be paid for—by you!—because of Obama.

- Obama ordered Frankenstein-like federal funding of Embryonic Stem cell research. Human beings will be created to be killed for the sake of "science."

- Obama is in the middle of rescinding the "conscience clause" regulations. Where this is headed is clear: Catholic Hospitals will be required to dispense abortions; Catholic health care workers will be required to be Obama's foot soldiers of death; like the soldiers under Herod's authority, health care workers will become merchants of death; OBGYN students will be forced to learn how to kill babies.

- Obama has pledged to sign FOCA, which could undo the prolife gains we have made over the last 20 years; Obama wants open ended child-killing.

In this "Fight:" Nothing is Sacred except the Sacred.
Notre Dame's pride is not sacred. President Obama's image is not sacred. Fr. Jenkins' job (Notre Dame President) is not sacred. The peace and quiet of Notre Dame's Directors is not sacred. "Calm dialogue" with the murderers of babies is not sacred.

Our Actions and Rhetoric—Equal to the Crime
We are opening an office in South Bend to live out these truths: Abortion is Murder; Obama supports murder; we must resist murder, and those who promote it. The love of life DEMANDS that we "fight" to stop this betrayal of God and babies.

Germany Revisited
After prominent pro-life leader Penny Lea had spoken one night, an elderly man approached her and gave her his testimony. This is his story:
"I lived in Germany during the Nazi holocaust. I considered myself a

Christian. I attended church since I was a small boy. We had heard the stories of what was happening to the Jews. But like most people today in this country, we tried to distance ourselves from the reality of what was really taking place. What could anyone do to stop it?

A railroad track ran behind our small church, and each Sunday morning we would hear the whistle from a distance and then the clacking of the wheels oving over the track. We became disturbed when on Sunday we noticed cries coming from the train as it passed by. We grimly realized that the train was carrying Jews. They were like cattle in those cars!

Week after week that train whistle would blow. We would dread to hear the sound of those old wheels because we knew that the Jews would begin to cry out to us as they passed our church. It was so terribly disturbing! We could do nothing to help these poor miserable people, yet their screams tormented us. We knew exactly at what time that whistle would blow, and we decided the only way to keep from being so disturbed by the cries was to start singing our hymns. By the time that train came rumbling past the church yard, we were singing at the top of our voices. If some of the screams reached our ears, we'd just sing a little louder until we could hear them no more. Years have passed and no one talks about it much anymore, but I still hear that train whistle in my sleep. I can still hear them crying out for help. God forgive all of us who called ourselves Christians, yet did nothing to intervene.

Now, so many years later, I see it happening all over again in America. God forgive you as Americans, for you have blocked out the screams of millions of your own children. The holocaust is here. The response is the same as it was in my country—SILENCE!"   Where was the Shepherd?

A little baby boy we named Baby Malachi, was found frozen in a jar with three other children at an abortion mill in Dallas, Texas, in February 1993. We were stunned when we found him. There were jars upon jars of frozen children in that abortion mill. Rhonda Mackey, our executive secretary at the time, brought this one jar out and asked me what we should do with it. I had no idea, but I instinctively knew we could not leave it there. We brought the jar to Dr. McCarty, a wonderful Ob-Gyn in Dallas, who put the pieces of this baby and the others back together. The entire process was put on video as Dr. McCarty and all who were present wept at the reconstruction of these precious children.

The life that was once there was now gone forever. It became apparent to all of us that God had given us these children, one in particular, to show to the entire world the horror of abortion. One picture can speak louder than a truckload of words. We prayed, and asked God to allow this little boy to speak to our nation.

We remembered the scripture in Hebrews 11:4: "…he still speaks, even though he is dead." It was upon a very specific revelation from our Lord that we had the picture of one baby blown up to poster size. Rhonda asked me if she might have the privilege of naming this little baby boy. She prayed, and God

gave her the name that this child would become known by all over the world—Malachi! *Malachi means, "My messenger."*

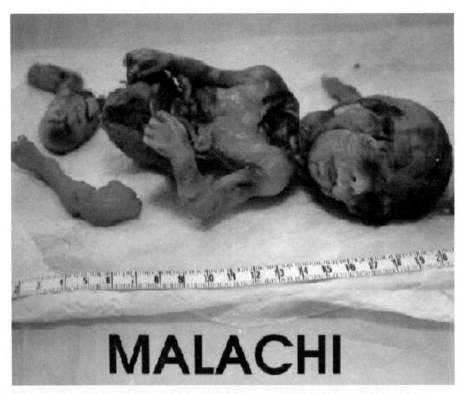

MALACHI

9

WHAT DOES IT MEAN TO BE A PRO-LIFE CHRISTIAN?

For years now we have been saying that abortion is preeminently a Gospel issue. It is a physical manifestation of the battle between two seeds—the *"seed of the serpent"* versus the *"seed of the woman"* Genesis 3:15.

Because this is true, there can be no compromise, no "reaching across the aisle," no "middle ground" in the abortion battle. Neither side will tolerate the other. When one chooses sides here, he is really choosing between God and the devil—between life and death! This battle has been raging through the pages of the Bible and the pages of history since the beginning of time. The *"seed of the serpent"* is in absolute rebellion against Almighty God and His Law. The *"seed of the woman"* is in agreement with Almighty God and His Law.

Every person on this earth must choose to be on one side or the other, there is no "in between." What one perceives the battle to be will determine how he fights it!

Education: If you perceive abortion to be primarily an educational issue, then you will do all that you can to educate people, helping them realize that life begins at conception. The problem is, that many in our nation already know this fact, but they believe a mother's right to choose trumps a child's right to live. It isn't about education!

Politics: If you perceive abortion to be primarily a political issue, then you will spend your time and money attempting to elect Republicans to make abortion illegal once again. However, politics is the art of compromise. To be successful, you must compromise God's Word to get His work done. This is never a good idea! It isn't about politics!

Economics: If you perceive abortion to be primarily an economic issue, then you will do all that you can to help those seeking an abortion to find financial help to see their baby to term and beyond. The problem is that most mothers seeking abortion just want to get it over with and get on with their lives. It isn't about finances!

Compassion: If you perceive abortion to be a compassion issue, then you will do all that you can to set up crisis pregnancy centers so that those seeking abortion instead choose life. The problem is that over 80% of the patients seen in crisis pregnancy centers are not abortion minded. Those seeking abortions don't go to crisis pregnancy centers. It isn't about compassion!

Gospel: If, however, you perceive abortion to be a Gospel issue, then you will call the Church of Jesus Christ into the streets to stand in the gap on behalf of pre-born children. If it is a battle between the *"seed of the serpent"* and the *"seed of the woman,"* only the Church of Jesus Christ can crush the head of the serpent. The gates of hell cannot prevail against her! Abortion is preeminently a Gospel issue!

If this is true, we Christians must confess that we have been wrong for the past 30 years in our fight against abortion. We must confess that, though well intentioned, we have failed to love our neighbor as our self. We must confess that we have lost sight of the spiritual nature of this battle and how it must be won. We have fought for the lives of children on every venue (educational, political, economic, compassionate, etc.) except this one. We have educated America about the sanctity of life. We have plunged into the political realm, electing Republican and conservative mercenaries to fight our battles for us. We have given financially, over and over again, to help mothers in crisis pregnancies. We have established crisis pregnancy centers. Unfortunately, we have not struck at the root of the problem.

It is only as the praying, proclaiming, praising Church of Jesus Christ allows her theology to become biography at local abortion mills in every city, that the battle may be won! The *"seed of the serpent"* is at war with *"the seed of the woman."* This is the battle!

Abortion is one of its most horrible physical manifestations. The devil is robbing, killing, and destroying God's heritage (children, Ps. 127) while we sit by trying to educate, negotiate, buy off, or be compassionate with God's sworn enemy. We have done everything but fight the devil and his lies with the Word of God.

The only entity ordained by God to crush the head of this serpent is the Church of Jesus Christ. It is time that we lived up to our high calling. Theology must become biography in the streets. The gates of hell cannot prevail. Abortion will come to an end in America when the Church of Jesus Christ makes up her mind it will come to an end—not one second sooner!

Flip Benham Director, Operation Rescue; Operation Save America

Many have asked if God will judge America. They have asked if we have gone too far to avoid God's terrible and final judgment. Let's face it. We have mercilessly killed over 50 million little baby boys and girls. We have thrown God out of school, banished Him from the schoolyard, and ripped His Ten Commandments from the walls of our schools. We have called what is evil good and what is good evil and we do not even know how to blush.

We have shaken our fist in the face of Almighty God, expecting the offended deity to bless us in the midst of our dismissing Him. Billy Graham said it well, "If God does not judge America, He is going to have to apologize to Sodom and Gomorrah."

God has already judged America and is presently judging her now, desiring that we return to Him. He has given us warning after warning through prophetic utterance, signs, and judgments. God's heart for America is most perfectly expressed in His words to the church of Laodicea:

"Those whom I love, I rebuke and discipline. So be earnest and repent. Here I am! I stand at the door and knock. If anyone hears my voice and opens the door, I will come in and eat with him, and he with me" (Rev 3:19-20).

"The wrath of God is being revealed from heaven against all the godlessness and wickedness of men who suppress the truth by their wickedness...' (Romans 1:18).

1. Islam, Red China, and North Korea are not our problem. They are signs and judgments from God. "Therefore the Lord was angry with His people... and their foes ruled over them" (Ps 106:40-41).

2. The fact that airplanes, flown by Islamic terrorists, smashed into buildings is not our problem. It is a sign and judgment from God. "I will set My face against you so that you will be defeated by your enemies; those that hate you will rule over you, and you will flee even when no one is pursuing you" (Lev 26:17).

3. Abortion is not our problem. It is a sign and judgment from God. "...but Ephraim will bring out their children to the slayer" (Hos 9:13).

4. Losing our kids to drugs, gangs, murder, and suicide is not our problem. It is a sign and judgment from God. "Even if they rear children, I will bereave them of every one..." (Hos 9:12).

5. Kids killing kids is not our problem. It is a sign and judgment from God. "...bloodshed follows bloodshed. Because of this the land mourns..." (Hos 4:2-3). "...Since you did not hate bloodshed, bloodshed will pursue you" (Ezek 35:6).

6. Homosexuality is not our problem. It is a sign and judgment from God. "They exchanged the truth of God for a lie...Because of this, God gave them over to shameful lusts..." (Rom 1:25-26).

7. Rampant crime is not our problem. It is a sign and judgment from God. "...No one could go about his business safely because of his enemy, for I had turned every man against his neighbor" (Zech 8:10).

8. Bad laws and statutes are not our problem. They are a sign and judgment from God. "...because they had not obeyed my laws...I also gave them over to statutes that were not good and laws they could not live by..." (Ezek 20:24-25).

9. The fact that God's people have become waffling compromisers or conservatives, unwilling to stand on the Word of God, is not our problem. It is a sign and judgment from God. "The men of Ephraim, though armed with bows, turned back on the day of battle..." (Ps 78:9).

10. Becoming a society of "victims" and blaming others is not our problem. It is a sign and judgment from God. "...The fathers have eaten sour grapes and the children's teeth are set on edge." (Jer 31:29).

11. The incredible number of lawsuits strangling our judicial system is not our problem. It is a sign and judgment from God. "They make many promises, take false oaths...therefore lawsuits spring up like poisonous weeds in a plowed field" (Hos 10:4).

12. The idea that "money can fix anything" is not our problem. It is a sign and judgment from God. "…but money is the answer for everything" (Eccl 10:19).

13. The fact that we do not have men of courage and principle is not our problem. It is a sign and judgment from God. "I will make boys their officials; mere children will govern them" (Isa 3:4).

14. The fact that radical feminists are moving into positions of great power is not our problem. It is a sign and judgment from God. "Youths oppress my people, women rule over them…your guides lead you astray, they turn you from the path" (Isa 3:12).

15. The fact that our women are now placed in military combat units is not our problem. It is a sign and judgment from God. "Look at your troops—they are all women! The gates of your land are all open to the enemy…" (Nahum 3:13).

16. Gay Pride Days and the blatant homosexual agenda are not our problem. They are a sign and judgment from God. "The look on their faces testifies against them; they parade their sin like Sodom; they do not hide it…" (Isa 3:9).

17. AIDS is not our problem. It is a sign and judgment from God. "Men committed indecent acts with other men, and received in themselves the due penalty for their perversion" (Rom 1:27).

18. The fact that the true prophet is not welcomed in today's church is not our problem. It is a sign and judgment from God. "…the prophet is considered a fool, the inspired man a maniac…snares await him on all his paths, and hostility in the house of his God" (Hos 9:7-8).

19. The fact that many pastors preach only positive, "seeker friendly" messages is not our problem. It is a sign and judgment from God. "They dress the wound of my people as though it were not serious. 'Peace, peace,' they say, when there is no peace" (Jer 6:14).

20. The fact that God's people in the American church demand only positive

messages is not our problem. It is a sign and judgment from God. "The prophets prophesy lies, the priests rule by their own authority, and my people love it this way..." (Jer 5:31).

21. The fact that "my rights, my body, my choice" has become the mantra of the day is not our problem. It is a sign and judgment from God. "In those days Israel had no king; everyone did as he saw fit" (Jdg 21:25).

22. The fact that senseless violence is increasing in the streets is not our problem. It is a sign and judgment from God. "Violence has grown into a rod to punish wickedness..." (Ezek 7:11).

23. The fact that our courts acquit the guilty (Michael Jackson) and condemn the innocent (Terri Schiavo) is not our problem. It is a sign and judgment from God. "...they not only continue to do these very things but also approve of those who practice them" (Rom 1:32).

24. The fact that our "imperial judiciary" has lost all sense of justice is not our problem. It is a sign and judgment from God. "Acquitting the guilty and condemning the innocent—the Lord detests them both" (Pr 17:15).

25. The fact that abortion, homosexuality, Islam, gambling, and pornography are being praised in our courts is not our problem. It is a sign and judgment from God. "Those who forsake the law praise the wicked..." (Pr 28:4).

26. The fact that street violence, domestic violence, child abuse, infanticide, and euthanasia are on the rise is not our problem. They are a sign and judgment from God. "In the streets the sword will make them childless. In their homes terror will reign. Young men and young women will perish, infants and gray haired men" (Dt 32:25).

27. The fact that injustice reigns in our courts is not our problem. It is a sign and judgment from God. "When a land falls into the hands of the wicked, He blindfolds its judges. If it is not He, then who is it" (Job 9:24)?

28. The fact that the prophets are blowing the trumpet in America to fight the Gospel battle and no one shows up is not our problem. It is a sign and judgment from God. "Though they blow the trumpet and get everything

ready, no one will go into battle, for my wrath is upon the whole crowd"
(Ezek 7:14).

29. The fact that God Himself has become our enemy is our problem. It is a
sign and judgment from Him. "Yet they rebelled and grieved His Holy
Spirit. So He turned and became their enemy and He Himself fought
against them" (Isa 63:10).

America was birthed as a "city set on a hill," whose foundations were built
upon the precepts of God's Word. Our Pilgrim Forefathers and our Founding
Fathers certainly believed this to be true. America therefore, has a responsibility
to Almighty God and to the world to let His light shine forth to the utter ends
of the earth. We have failed in our responsibility. God is lovingly calling us to
return to Him and fulfill our purpose as a nation. His judgments upon our land
are signs that we must repent and call upon His Name (2 Chronicles 7:14).

For those who doubt that God would judge America, we need only look
upon the prevalent writings, sermons, and speeches of Civil War days.

"Every master of slaves is a petty tyrant. They bring the judgment of
heaven upon a country. As nations cannot be rewarded or punished in the next
world, they must be in this … Providence punishes national sins with national
calamities." George Mason "On many a defeated field there was a voice louder
than the thundering of a cannon. It was the voice of God, crying, 'Let my
people go.' We were all very slow in realizing it was God's voice, but after
many humiliating defeats the nation came to believe it a great and solemn
command. Great multitudes begged and prayed that I might answer God's
voice by signing the Emancipation Proclamation, and I did it, believing we
never should be successful in the great struggle unless the God of Battles has
been on our side." Abraham Lincoln.

Flip Benham
National Director, Operation Save America; Operation Rescue

10

THE CONGREGATION OF THE DEAD (NO SHEPHERDS?)

The man that wandereth out of the way of understanding shall remain in the congregation of the dead (Proverbs 21:16).

America is a dying country. I hate to be the one to break the news to you, but America is a dead man walking. The once great "shining city on a hill" is gasping for breath. Everywhere you turn you are faced with the harsh truth that the death rattle has begun. We are a dying people controlled by a dying government, infected with the dead leadership of dead men, who chew on a dead gospel served-up in dead churches, by dead pastors living out a dead faith.

The stench of death is permeating our society. How could this possibly be? America, has wandered "out of the way of understanding." Make no mistake about it; America is dying of spiritual starvation. We are the victims of spiritual <u>bulimia</u>, willingly vomiting out all that would nourish us. America is a congregation of the dead.

We have no one to blame but the Church. I know that makes many of you nervous as you cling to your "<u>dead faith full of dead works</u>" believing that God is pleased with your apathy towards the spiritual condition of this nation. You, my Christian friends, are complicit in the spiritual coup that has swept over America. Compromise is the birthing ground of sin. Savorless salt producing good-for-nothing Christianity.

It is easy to blame the sinner as he proudly gallivants his debauchery for all to see. But it is the "compromise of the converted" that has paved the way for our national suicide. It is not the bold sinner that has destroyed our nation, but the "Silent Saint" <u>ashamed to speak the Truth</u>. And make no mistake about it…we have only ourselves to blame. We have willingly "wandered out of the way of <u>understanding</u>." We followed folly, "<u>changed the truth of God into a lie</u> and are reaping the whirlwind from our unwillingness to <u>contend for the</u>

74

<u>Truth</u>. Silence isn't golden, it's yellow.

We are a nation of liars, following liars, believing liars, and celebrating liars. Jesus said "<u>The words that I speak unto you, they are spirit, and they are life.</u> We have rejected His words, and we have rejected His life. "<u>Sanctify them through thy truth: thy word is truth.</u>"

Freddie Mae and Freddie Mac are the vomit of America's bulimia. "*For they have sown the wind, and they shall reap the whirlwind: it hath no stalk; the bud shall yield no meal: if so be it yield, the strangers shall swallow it up* (Hosea 8:7).

Strangers are swallowing us up. How else can you explain the impotence of the American Church? Only a fool would deny the cause of our malnutrition. We have belched out <u>the bread of life</u>. <u>Professing ourselves to be wise we became fools</u>. No wonder our nation is the congregation of the dead.

As is our custom, my wife and I were doing our daily devotions this morning and our Scripture reading was <u>II Thessalonians 2</u>. "*And with all deceivableness of unrighteousness in them that perish; because they received not the love of the truth, that they might be saved. And for this cause God shall send them strong delusion, that they should believe a lie: That they all might be damned who believed not the truth, but had pleasure in unrighteousness.*"

Much of America is Christian in Name Only. (CHINO) We wear Jesus like a merit badge from the Boy Scouts. But for most Americans church membership is no different than membership in the local Moose Lodge or the American Legion. It is a social structure where like-minded folks get together for fellowship. Like the <u>Shriners</u>, the Church is a club for do-gooders who want to shine their "Christian Medals" for their friends to see.

Almighty God warned us. "*See, I have set before thee this day life and good, and death and evil; In that I command thee this day to love the LORD thy God, to walk in his ways, and to keep his commandments and his statutes and his judgments, that thou mayest live and multiply: and the LORD thy God shall bless thee in the land whither thou goest to possess it. But if thine heart turn away, so that thou wilt not hear, but shalt be drawn away, and worship other gods, and serve them; I denounce unto you this day, that ye shall surely perish, and that ye shall not prolong your days upon the land, whither thou passest over Jordan to go to possess it. I call heaven and earth to record this day against you, that I have set before you life and death, blessing and cursing: therefore choose life, that both thou and thy seed may live*" (<u>Deuteronomy 30</u>). <u>For the wages of sin is death; but the gift of God is eternal life through Jesus Christ our Lord.</u>

We have rejected God, rejected His Truth, and rejected His Son. We have embraced death, celebrate death, and subsidize death. We are a congregation of the dead. Our government is corrupt because our people are corrupt. Our people are corrupt because our churches are corrupt. Most serve mammon and give lip-service to God. Pastors beg the government to permit them to preach what God has commanded them to say. No man can serve two masters.

"*Come now, and let us reason together, saith the LORD: though your sins be as scarlet, they shall be as white as snow; though they be red like crimson, they shall be as wool. If ye be willing and obedient, ye shall eat the good of the land: But if ye refuse and rebel, ye shall be devoured with the sword: for the mouth of the LORD hath spoken it. How is the faithful city become an harlot! it was full of judgment; righteousness lodged in it; but now murderers*" (Isaiah 1).

Our faithful city has become a harlot. II Chronicles 7:14 is a popular verse, IF MY PEOPLE…it seems so easy and simple. But rarely do I hear the companion to that verse quoted…the IF NOT of God's conditional promise. How many of you are familiar with the IF NOT of II Chronicles 7:19? *But if ye turn away, and forsake my statutes and my commandments, which I have set before you, and shall go and serve other gods, and worship them; Then will I pluck them up by the roots out of my land which I have given them; and this house, which I have sanctified for my name, will I cast out of my sight, and will make it to be a proverb and a byword among all nations. And this house, which is high, shall be an astonishment to every one that passeth by it; so that he shall say, Why hath the LORD done thus unto this land, and unto this house? And it shall be answered, Because they forsook the LORD God of their fathers, which brought them forth out of the land of Egypt, and laid hold on other gods, and worshipped them, and served them: therefore hath he brought all this evil upon them.*"

Read it closely. It is God doing the plucking, God doing the casting out, and God making it a byword among all the nations. But the "elected officials" and the men of God called to hold them accountable will ask "Why has the Lord done this to our nation?" And it shall be answered "because they forsook the LORD God of their fathers…therefore HATH HE brought all of this evil upon them."

God is judging America my friends. Fifty million babies aborted, sodomy in the streets, and the purging of His name…."*I tremble for my country when I reflect that God is just, that His justice cannot sleep forever.*" Thomas Jefferson.

The alleged-deist Thomas Jefferson was ten-times the Christian most evangelicals are today and the Baptists wanted to run him out of office. "*… therefore hath he brought all this evil upon them.*"

—Coach Dave Daubenmire

11

FEAR, PRIDE, AND GREED

I have just returned from a ten day speaking tour of the state of Missouri. For the past few years a group of us have been offering our services to churches around America who are willing to pull their head's out of the sand and take a good, hard look at what is really going on in America. I could tell you that we are speaking to overflow crowds and that America is being turned upside down by the truth that we are sharing, but that would be as phony as the "stimulus package." We are faithful to go, but sometimes have a hard time finding a church willing to open their doors to us.

This "Shake The Nation" tour was no exception. I know that this may sound arrogant but the Gospel-Truth that our "traveling-road show" delivers is something that every Christian needs to hear. We present the Biblical perspective on the schools, our Constitution, the condition of the American Church, abortion, communism, the homosexual agenda, the 501 C 3 muzzle, and a general overview of a Christian Worldview.

Invariably, we will find a courageous pastor (A true Shepherd) who is more committed to building his people than he is to building a church, who opens his doors and welcomes us in. God bless those faithful men of God, many who are un-paid pastors, who understand their charge to be "watchmen on the wall."

During last week's tour, as five of us squeezed into a van and traveled nearly 300 miles between Friday night in Branson and Saturday evening in St. Louis, I bemoaned the fact that none of the larger churches would have us in. But we fight the fact that most pastors more resemble gate-keepers than they do watchmen. They do all they can to shield themselves, and their congregations, from the reality of the world outside their stained-glassed fortresses, and their obligation to defend the faith. "What is up with the pastors?" one of our group wondered out loud. "What is the reason that they won't get involved?"

Dr. Gregory Thompson, the leader of our pack, never batted an eye as he turned from the front passenger seat and answered, "There are three reasons...

fear, pride, and greed." I don't know if anyone has so squarely hit the nail on the head. Our group comes for free. All we ask is that the churches take an offering to try and meet our expenses. We sleep on couches, share beds, or on the floor in a sleeping bag, and we are fed by volunteer families in each location. It costs a church less than a marriage seminar, a financial freedom conference, or a celebrity speaker that teaches ten ways to make ten-thousand dollars in ten weeks.

Soft Christian-sounding programs are all the rage. The feel-good gospel always packs them in. But our message is different. We inform the flock, present a challenge, and demand a response. In a church-community that thrives off of spiritual welfare, the idea that our Faith requires a Christian to do that with which he is uncomfortable is almost unthinkable. After all, Jesus came to serve us, don't you know? Most Christians are more likely to be stricken by bed-sores from the padded pews than they are from the attacks of the enemy. Our pastors are to blame. Dr. Thompson is right. They are paralyzed by the Devil's trinity of fear, pride and greed. Professional Christians are selling out this nation.

Most pastors are cowards. At a time when the "faith of our Fathers" has never been under more of an attack, they are missing in action. When America is crying for bold, courageous leadership our pulpits are filled with meek men who preach weak in-offensive messages. They fear the flock, the government, bold men, and public opinion. They are content to allow their people to perish because of their fear of speaking the truth. How else can you explain their silence in the face of the thievery taking place in Washington?

Or perhaps it is their pride. The idea that a hearty band of "Christian Activists" could teach Dr. Know It All something regarding "the Faith" is almost insulting. After all, he spent years in seminary, read thousands of commentaries on the Scriptures and has "built a church" attended by thousands of uninformed sheep. What could this group of "zealots" possibly teach him about herding sheep? And how would he explain it to the other CEO's at the local "ministerial association?" Meanwhile, the sheep are perishing as the shepherd slumbers. But it is probably their greed that encumbers them the most. Have you watched the Trinity Broadcasting Network lately? When was the last time you saw a Christian leader on that program speak out against the un-Godly actions of our "ministers of God" in the District of Criminals? When was the last time you heard them speak out about the slaughter of innocent pre-born children?

No man can serve two masters and "butts and bucks" are what drives most ministries. Heaven forbid they would do anything to risk their tax-exemption or offend the fat-cat donor after whom the new "ministry center" will be built. The Christian soldiers are in retreat because the Christian army is a headless-horseman. We are an infantry without generals, and those who should be leading resent those who want to. This has happened before. "When Adolf Hitler came to power in Germany in 1933, he scornfully dismissed the Church and her pastors as an irrelevant force which posed no threat to the Nazi agenda for that great nation. 'I promise you,' he boasted to his inner circle, 'that if I wish to, I could destroy the Church in just a few years. It is hollow, it is rotten and false through and through. One push, and the whole structure would collapse. We should trap the preachers,' he said, 'by their notorious greed and self-indulgence. We shall thus be able to settle everything with them in perfect peace and harmony. I shall give them a few years' reprieve. Why should we quarrel? They will swallow anything in order to keep their material advantage. The parsons will be made to dig their own graves; they will betray their God for us. They will betray anything for the sake of their miserable jobs and incomes.'"

It was only sixty years ago that Hitler rose to power in Germany. He did so with the blessings of the clergy. I, for one, do not want to wait for our leaders to lead. A brief study of history will show where we will end up. "In the winter of 1943, a group of university students in Munich, calling themselves The White Rose, began a desperate effort to awaken the young people of that nation to the malignant evil that had engulfed their country. Led by a 25-year old student named Hans Scholl, they distributed leaflets across the campus in a doomed effort to provoke resistance to the Hitler regime. Six leaflets were written. Number Four in the series included this desperate plea, a plea which could have been written today, and a plea which could have been addressed to us. Scholl wrote, "Everywhere, at all times of greatest trial, men have appeared, prophets and saints, who cherished their freedom, who preached the one God and who with His help brought the people to a reversal of their downward course. I ask you now, as a Christian, wrestling for the preservation of your greatest treasure: Why do you hesitate? Why are you inclined toward intrigue, calculation and procrastination? Are you hoping that someone else will raise his arm in your defense? God has given you the strength! God has given you the will to fight! We must attack the evil now, where it is strongest!" Pastor Martin Niemöller was one of the brave Christians who stood against the Nazis. It cost him his life. The morning after he was arrested a Chaplain making his rounds found Niemöllar sitting behind bars. ""My brother!" he exclaimed.

"What did you do? Why are you here?" Niemöller, never at a loss for words, immediately reacted. "My brother, given what's happened in our country, why aren't you here?"

This nation is in crisis as our Christian leadership worship an un-holy trinity of fear, pride, and greed. We would love to visit you. If you are one of those courageous pastors, or if you go to a church led by such a man, we would love to stand with you. Call us at 740-507-3211 or 417-894-5768.

12

A SUBTLE SIN—EASY TO IGNORE (ALL PEOPLE OF GOD LISTEN!)

The SIN of PRIDE. When Satan caused the fall in the Garden of Eden, he appealed to three areas of weakness within mankind. Those areas of weakness are described in Scripture in the book of John. *"For all that is in the world, the lust of the flesh, and the lust of the eyes, and the pride of life, is not of the Father, but is of the world"* (1 John 2:16).

(Authors note: Shepherds, understand that we speak of ourselves also, in the following, and all of us must put on our armor, praying and asking for protection against this evil.)

Our sin nature is not God centered, it is prideful and self-centered and it strives to please itself. Words that help us to understand pride are arrogance, conceit, smugness, and self importance. The first step to victory over pride is when we recognize and then deal with this reality. The way to do that is to understand that we overcome this sin, and other sins, through true repentance and faith in Jesus Christ and His finished work at the Cross. That is what gives the Holy Spirit the freedom to work in our heart. In a world full of pride and self-indulgence, we must be alert to the methods that Satan uses to trap us in this sin. One way he uses pride is to attempt to make us think we are more important than we are and to build our self-esteem. The flesh feeds on that!

David, inspired by the Holy Spirit, shatters our self-esteem when he says that at our best we are full of pride. *"Every man at his best state is altogether vanity"* (Psalm 39:5). Jeremiah tells us that our *"heart is deceitful above all things, and desperately wicked"* (Jeremiah 17:9).

Again, we do not have the power within us to overcome: we must yield to the Holy Spirit who will help us prevail over our fallen nature.

We learn from David as he spoke of dependence on the Lord to overcome the sin of arrogance, "Who can understand his errors? Cleanse thou me from secret faults. Keep back thy servant also from presumptuous sins: let them not have dominion over me: then shall I be upright, and I shall be innocent from the great transgression. Let the words of my mouth, and the meditation of my heart, be acceptable in thy sight. O LORD, my strength and my redeemer" (Psalm 19;12-14).

Shepherds, do you really want to get a handle on what God wants of you? Then understand these verses instruct us not only to seek the Lord for cleansing from sins we may not know about, but they are also a plea to God for protection from presumptuous sins that are produced from pride and self-confidence. Pride can blind us into wrongly thinking we are innocent of sin.

Pride is our staunch enemy and can blind us to genuine repentance. No doubt, it has taken many to hell over centuries because they would not humble themselves and repent.

Pride is a subtle sin and easy to ignore. It can manifest itself in many ways. Someone said pride is the parent sin of universe because it was what motivated Lucifer to rebel against God. As I have stated, pride causes us to please "self" rather than the Lord.

Pride fortifies man-centered religion, stiff-necked self-righteousness and self-help. This conceit will drive us to pray amiss out of a lust for the things of the world.

Pride is what drives Christians (& Shepherds) to appeal to, and be accepted by a fallen world. When our feelings are hurt or when we cannot forgive someone, it is the sin of pride coming through loud and clear.

Pride will drive us to favor some people over others. When snared in pride, as the Book of James tells us, we will look down on those dressed in poor shabby clothing, while we cater to those with flashy jewelry, and expensive attire (James 2:1-9).

If our issue is pride, we will toot our own horn and boast of our accomplishments. If we don't have any, we'll make something up! Arrogance always pays tribute to self.

Doing church today, in too many instances, and in varying degrees, has become a production where carnality reigns. It's often glitzy, extravagant, and rehearsed to make the flesh feel good. The Holy Spirit is grieved with it all. Multitudes of Christian Shepherds work hard to make proud sinners feel comfortable as they cater to their fallen state. The praise of men is always more important than the praise of God when we are out of fellowship with the Lord!

The height of pride is to think that we are okay when we are not! Jesus told lukewarm church members at the church of Laodicea to be zealous and repent. He said it was because they thought they didn't need anything (Author's note: does that statement hold true to any listening to this message, yes all of us, get on your knees and pray). Their blindness was incredible! He said, *"So then because thou art lukewarm, and neither cold nor hot, I will spew thee out of my mouth. Because thou sayest, I am rich, and increased with goods, and need of nothing; and knowest not that thou art wretched, and miserable and poor, and blind, and naked"* (Revelation 3:15-19).

Pride can blind us to the reality of our condition while we are deceived into thinking that we will stay in God's grace while we live in sin. Pride will lead us into completely false estimation of ourselves. *"Therefore let him who thinks he stands take heed lest he fall"* (1Corinthians 10:12). It was pride that drove the Pharisees, who thought they were in God's grace, to reject Jesus and crucify Him.

(Author's note, especially Notre Dame, yet all Shepherds, pray for ears to hear and eyes to see as this is brought to a close, each person struggles with pride to different degrees and many are blind to this, for your own walk with Jesus, for your own soul, for the souls of those that look to you, pray daily for forgiveness of this sin, ask to be delivered from this sin daily, ask the Lord right now to let you see your blindness about this, don't let pride stop you.)

If we consider how grievously short of the Glory of God we have come to have sinned against our merciful Lord, we have nothing to boast of. When we consider our hopeless situation before salvation and how great the sins we have been forgiven of, and the price Jesus paid for them, we have nothing to be proud of. It is all about Jesus and our Father who loved us enough, while we were yet sinners, to send Christ to die for our sins!

We should strive to yield to the Holy Spirit and allow Him to bring any pride we may have into submission. Our desire should be to make Jesus more important than we are. John the Baptist was speaking about Jesus when he said, *"He must increase, but I must decrease. He that comes from above is above all: he that is of the earth is earthly, and speaks of the earth; he that comes from heaven is above all"* (John 3:30-31).

R. L. Beasley, a close brother in Christ, publishes the Beacon out of Joplin, Missouri and he hit a home run as usual with this exhortation to all that claim the name of Christ, especially the Shepherds. Thank you R.L.

13

ARE CHRISTIANS HELPING SEND CHILDREN TO HELL?

Jesus said, *"All power is given unto me in heaven and earth. Go you therefore, and teach all nations, baptizing them in the name of the Father, and of the Son, and of the Holy Ghost: Teaching them to observe all things whatsoever I have commanded you: and, lo, I am with you always, even unto the end of the world. Amen"* (Matthew 28:18-20).

What are you waiting for? To know this and to say that you have been reborn, how does it hold that Shepherds and Christians do nothing? You might say, what do you mean, do nothing? We send some money to missions, we have wonderful committee meetings, we give food to the local pantry, we are involved in all the mercy ministries.

Yes, do the mercy ministries, but to know what to do and not do it, is it not said to be a sin, by God. As children's souls are at risk of going to hell for eternity and children are murdered daily, do you think that it will be a good idea to hang on to the thought that you will tell Jesus you fed the hungry, and clothed the naked, while children went to hell? Will Jesus tell many sleeping Christians to go over with the goats, He does not know you?

I judge none of your hearts, Jesus has given me a gift to love you, but you must judge yourself, before Jesus does. I do judge out of love, your actions or lack of. Look around you; do you not understand the times at all? Are you willing to hear a prophetic warning, or do you just want your best life now? Do you want the truth, or just to feel good.

Every pastor and priest that does not tell his flock to get their children out of the government schools is sinning and putting themselves at risk of going to hell for eternity. Every elder that does not warn the pastor and the people about getting out of the government schools is sinning and putting themselves at risk of going to hell for eternity. Every Christian sitting in the pews that does not warn the pastor and elders and the people setting in the pews to get their children out of the government schools is putting themselves at risk of going to hell for eternity.

The government school, yes government, because they are no longer public, as they indoctrinate the children in an ungodly and pagan environment full of lies, and socializing them to be good little comrades. Even though it was never meant biblically to put our children into a public school, at one time they at least tried to keep God a strong part of the education of the child so that they could recognize the counterfeit leaders we have in our government today, and would quickly put them out of service to the people.

Jesus told you to "Seek first HIS kingdom" and those going to His kingdom will love God with all their hearts, minds, souls, and strength, and love their neighbor as themselves. Do not say that you love Jesus if you are putting the children at risk for eternity in an indoctrination system that is against God, family, and country. As you sleep, the atheistic communists in our government will look for more and more ways to indoctrinate your children away from God and into their fold.

Please Shepherds, priests, pastors, elders, and Christians do not deceive yourselves, your children are at great risk when attending a government k-12 and a government college. And many of your so called Christian Colleges and schools have been infiltrated also. I know that many have made this Sacred Cow of government education an Idol, and those that understand the urgency for the children must pray for those with strongholds that keep them from seeing and hearing.

God Hates Workers of Iniquity

Many Humanists don't want God around because His commands limit their licentiousness. Liberal leaning people that claim Christ as their Savior, like the love and mercy part of Jesus, but hate and refute the justice part of God. They make God a liar so that they can call evil good and good evil, and become workers of iniquity who are pleased when others are convinced to participate and condone their sin.

The full counsel of God in Scripture is offensive to those that love sin more than God, and God hates those that know the government education system is promoted by workers of iniquity, and stay silent as His children are taught lies from the pit of hell. How long will the Shepherds in the church stay silent, with many pulpits hated by God, because they ignore what is being taught to the children in the government schools, they have indeed been disobedient, prideful, greedy, fearful, and silent.

The church must take a primary role in the minds of the children. Shepherds, if you are truly called, you have no excuse, and if you just took this as a job, you had better repent and run as fast as you can away from the pulpit and teaching the word of God. Those in the pews, remember, "Do not conform any longer to the pattern of this world, but be transformed by the renewing of your mind" (Romans 12:2).

14

WHAT DOES ABORTION, HOMOSEXUALITY, AND ISLAM HAVE IN COMMON?

They are all inspired by the same liar who has come to the earth to rob, kill, and destroy. All three are the beneficiaries of the marvelous freedoms and liberty we have in America. All three have violated these freedoms and perverted liberty—making it license. All three deny God and the truth of His Word. All three have entered into a pact with death. All three are often more rigorous in their devotion to false "gods" than "Christians" are devoted to the one true GOD. All three have a desperate need for the forgiveness found only through the blood of Christ. "Salvation is found in no one else, for there is no other Name under heaven given to men by which we must be saved" (Acts 4:12).

It is precisely for this reason that we come to you today, to share the love of Almighty God as expressed through His one and only son, Jesus Christ. "Do not hate your brother in your heart. Rebuke your neighbor frankly so you will not share in his guilt" (Leviticus 19:17). We are here as a living and gentle rebuke. Our Lord commands us in His Holy Scripture that, if we truly love our neighbor, we must tell him the truth. We are here to proclaim to you this day that Jesus Christ is God and apart from Him there is no other. To do or say any less would be hate!

Sincere Belief is no Substitute for Truth

The nineteen men who crashed airplanes into buildings and brought many innocent people to their untimely deaths may have sincerely believed that they were serving God, but they were sincerely wrong. If they could come back from the dead and speak to us today, they would reveal a horror that is beyond words to describe. Rather than joining 72 virgins as promised, they have found themselves in hell for eternity—one cannot even commit suicide to get out. It is eternal damnation! The truth of what one believes is far more important than how much he believes it. Truth is paramount!

Kamikaze pilots, on suicide missions for a false god (Japanese Emporer Hirihito), attempted to crash their airplanes into American ships. No one can doubt the sincerity and zeal of these young men who so carelessly gave their lives for an unworthy and untrue cause, but death and hell were their eternal reward. Those who boarded the Titanic sincerely believed that the ship would not sink. They were sincere in their belief, but their sincerity could not save them when the ship sank. What they believed was a lie. The ship could sink, and the ship did sink. Truth is paramount!

Since Mohammed's vision in the early seventh century, millions have been slaughtered by the lie of Islam. This false religion, birthed from the very pit of hell, has led to the eternal damnation of billions of precious people whom God loves that have been led astray from the one true God (Jesus Christ). No matter how sincere, no matter how committed, no matter how willing to die for "Allah," the result will forever be the same—eternal damnation! Believing a lie has severe consequences.

Our Failure to Rightly Represent Christ to You (Shepherds?)

Unfortunately, Christianity in America has become so feminized, weak, and limp -wristed that these lies (abortion, homosexuality, and Islam) have come to prevail in a nation that was established and made great on the manly bedrock of biblical Christianity. We, the Church of Jesus Christ in America, have failed to love our neighbors lost in Islam by not representing the true God of the Bible to them. We have thrown God out of our schools and banished Him from the schoolyard. We have allowed mothers and fathers to kill their children at a whim. We have allowed sexual lusts to run rampant. Murder fills our streets. Drugs steal our kids. And, not content with the pollution of our own nation, we have become a pipeline through which the whole world is being polluted. We do all of this, yet proclaim with our lying lips that Jesus Christ is our Lord!

The lives we live, the laws we pass, the example we have become have defiled God's Holy Name. For this we ask your forgiveness. But because we are false to the true and living God does not mean that He is false!

15

AMERICA WAS FOUNDED UPON THE PRINCIPLES OF CHRISTIANITY

It was not a group of Hindus, Muslims, and Christians that sailed across the Atlantic to the shores of the "New World" to begin a new nation where one was free to worship Almighty God (Jesus). It was those who loved Christ. It was upon the principles found in the Bible and the liberty found in Jesus Christ that the foundations of our nation were laid. Our Pilgrim forefathers viewed their lives as "stepping stones" upon which future generations could trod in the advancement of the Gospel of Christ. Our Founding Fathers placed their lives, their fortunes, their sacred honors safely in the hands of Jesus believing that "divine providence" alone would suffice in their battle for independence. Yes, America was founded and built by those following hard after Christ.

One of our Founding Fathers, Patrick Henry, put it this way: "It cannot be emphasized too often or too strongly that this nation was founded not by religionists but by Christians, not on religion but the Gospel of Jesus Christ. It is for this very reason that people of other faiths have been afforded prosperity, asylum, and freedom of worship."

If you are wondering why you are able to still freely worship a false god in this marvelous and free country you need only look to our LORD Jesus. He said, "Come unto me, all ye that labor and are heavy laden, and I will give you rest." Matthew 11:28. He doesn't demand His dogma to be forced upon you like Islamic Jihad. He bids you to come—you can choose to accept or reject Him.

This freedom is found only in a nation whose God is the LORD (YAHWEH). BLESSED IS THE NATION WHOSE GOD IS THE LORD "Blessed is the nation whose God is the LORD...." Ps. 33:12. The Hebrew word for LORD in this text is "YAHWEH." America has been blessed because our God is YAHWEH. Our nation is a bastion of liberty and freedom, the likes of which have never been seen on this earth, because YAHWEH is our God. The word YAHWEH is translated in English, I AM.

This Name for God, YAHWEH, was first revealed to Moses in Exodus 3:11-15 when Moses asked, "... and who should I say sent me?" God replied, "I AM,... say to them I AM sent you." It was by this Name, YAHWEH that God said He would be remembered forever, from generation to generation.

This Name was so sacred to the Jews that they removed the vowels (jots and tittles in Hebrew) and made it YHWH or the Tetragrammaton. They did not want to be guilty of taking God's Name in vain. Jesus, However, made one of the most startling statements ever uttered when He confronted the Jews in their religious hypocrisy: "Verily, verily, I say unto you, Before Abraham was, I AM." John 8:58. He used the Name, YAHWEH!

This so stunned the monotheistic Jews that they tried to stone Him right there. Jesus told them that He was God! He told them that He was, is, and always will be YAHWEH! Hear this my friends, it is Jesus and Jesus alone who is GOD! Not Allah, as interpreted by Mohammed, not Gautama Buddha, not Krishna, not the god in me nor the god in the tree.

It is Jesus who made and makes this nation great. Ask yourself why people from all over the world come here. There is something about the liberty and freedom to pursue the very purpose for which one is born that makes America different from any other nation on the earth: "... and where the spirit of the Lord is there is liberty."

It is the Lord of liberty (Jesus) that you seek. It is He that draws so many to this nation. He is the one and only true God. He bids you to come unto Him, confess your sins, and find the forgiveness that only He can give. It is our prayer that you will come to experience this liberty in your own heart. Jesus said, "...you will _know_ the truth and the truth shall set you free." John 8:32.

Thank you Flip Benham, may Jesus continue to speak his Truth through you. Director, Operation Save America; Operation Rescue National

16

DO YOU ATTEND A STATE CONTROLLED CHURCH?

Senior Devil, *"One of our great allies at present is the Church itself. Do not misunderstand me, I do not mean the Church as we see her spread out through all time and space and rooted in eternity, terrible as an army with banners. That, I confess is a spectacle which makes our boldest tempters uneasy. But fortunately it is quite invisible to these humans."*

Screwtape, a senior devil, instructing a junior devil on how to tempt and trap humans. C.S. Lewis, The Screwtape Letters.

Do you attend a State controlled Church? If I may, let me ask you to take a simple quiz to find out:

1. Does your church have By-laws or a church constitution that it is governed by?
2. Does your church elect Trustees, a President, or a Chairman of the Board?
3. Is your church Tax Exempt with the I.R.S.?
4. Is your church incorporated within your state?
5. Does your church belong to a denomination that is incorporated or tax exempt?

If you answered YES to any of these questions, then the STATE dictates to your church what it can and cannot say.

You may not have been able to answer many of the above questions off the top of your head. The majority of people who attend church rarely know anything about the way their church is governed. If you were able to answer some or all of the questions with a "yes," then what you are about to ready may shock you; at least I hope it gets your attention. Churches have by-laws or constitutions because the state demands that ALL "incorporated churches" be governed by one.

When a church incorporates, it literally takes a corporate law book and lays it along side the Bible and declares that the State is now the senior partner in the governing of this union between the Church and State. To incorporate means to blend two things into one, so that the church will no longer be what it once was, it now becomes a Church Inc. My friend, we have no right to take the Church of our Lord Jesus Christ, which He purchased with His blood, and unite it with the State through incorporation. 2 Corinthians 6:14-17 says, "Do not be bound together with unbelievers; for what partnership have righteousness and lawlessness, or what fellowship have light with darkness? Or what harmony has Christ with Belial, or what has a believer in common with unbelievers? Or what agreement has the temple of God with idols? For we are the temple of the living God; just as God said, I will dwell among them and walk among them; and I will be their God, and they shall be My people. Therefore, come out from among them and be separate, says the Lord."

Every week millions of believers sit comfortably in their pews to worship and watch their cleric perform. We sing our favorite hymns, do our church duties, and for some, study our Bibles. I mean, it is somewhat comforting to view a decaying world from the distant safety of our sanctuaries while we strive to strengthen our own personal relationship with God. Not that striving for personal holiness is wrong; it is central to the Christian life. But the Christian faith doesn't stop on an individual level.

When believers shout, "Jesus is Lord," we refer to His rule over our own lives, of course, but we are also acknowledging His sovereignty over all He has created, especially His Church, the Body! That means we have the awesome responsibility of asserting that rule, of proclaiming His truth, in a world that is scornfully asking Pilate's timeless question: "What is truth?"

We cannot sit back in our sanctuaries and refuse to take up this challenge. We cannot forgo the corporate consequences of Jesus' Lordship. For we alone can provide the answer and point a weary skeptical culture to the ultimate and only reality, Jesus Christ Himself. His body, His Church, is charged with the obligation to defend His truth. As the Apostle Paul described in his letter to Timothy, the Church is to be "the pillar and support of the truth." That which raises up the truth and makes it visible to the world. That means we must know the truth. So we must ask ourselves the very important question: If the Church we attend on a regular basis is a "state controlled church," is it really the church Jesus Christ died for?

Please remember that the church is not a democracy and never can be. We can change the rules and practices and sing new hymns and use different styles of worship. We can change forms, but not the foundations! For the church is authoritarian! It is ruled over by Christ the Head and governed by a constitution (the Bible) that cannot be ignored or amended. "The solid foundation of God stands, having this seal: 'The Lord knows those who are His.' and 'Let everyone who names the name of Christ depart from iniquity'" (2 Timothy 2:19).

I close this with a quote, *"The Church must be reminded that it is not the master or servant of the state, but rather the conscience of the state. It must be the guide and the critic of the state, and never its tool. If the church does not recapture its prophetic zeal, it will become an irrelevant social club without moral or spiritual authority."*
Dr. Martin Luther King Jr

Christian Shepherds change your actions or change your name.

Pastor Mark Kiser is another warrior Shepherd for our Lord and Savior Jesus Christ, who is searching for a remnant of true Shepherds. Because of your silence and fear, you have let other evils come amongst the sheep that deceive those that believe the truth that indeed, Jesus is God.

17

JESUS IS GOD

Jesus is God. I struggled to find an understanding, a counter—a clever stroke to the repeated "We serve the same God," that the terrorists in charge of the mosque kept iterating, (and the Shepherds were not teaching).

It was quite unsettling. When faced with a philosophical idea that I can't grasp, or to be overwhelmed by a computer genius who keeps saying, "it's so easy," my brain seizes, freezes. It's a sensory state I do not like.

A number of pals and I had gone to the "local" mosque to find out what makes Muslims tick. Unbeknownst to me, to any of us—the imam, the leader of this mosque just happened to be the number one Muslim in the United States. He was so powerful that he had actually conned the President of the United States with a tactic of philosophical hide the pea equivocation.

This imam stood before us and read from the Gospel of John in English and read the first verse of the first chapter of John and said, "In the beginning was the word and the word was with God and the word was Allah. You see, my friends—this is from your very own missionaries and it's how they teach that your God is our God."

Very clever I thought—and this is exactly how he got the President of the United States and the Secretary of State conned to believe indeed, the God of Islam is the God of the Holy Bible.

I know you are shaking your head and thinking how silly and sophomoric that this could throw me for a loop.

I heard this repeated frequently over the 2 hours or so of brain washing from this Imam who bragged he had to leave soon to catch a plane for Riyadh, Saudi Arabia to meet directly with the King of Saudi Arabia. While I knew we were in a mosque, I had no idea we were in a terrorist mosque—and certainly no idea that I would discover soon it is THE terrorist Central Head Quarters of not just the U.S.A—but also Canada and Mexico.

Later when we asked the number one terrorist of America what he would do with his sins, a man from his mosque charged us, stopping alongside this Number 1 Terrorist, slammed into the chain link fence separating us and screamed, "I am glad they blew up the World Trade Center. I am glad they killed all those Americans.

But right now—this first day, I listened to this accomplished con artist—not aware just how powerful he was—I wondered, How could I counter this refrain of "We worship the same God, and actually be able to witness to the Muslims of this mosque."

We had reached an impasse with this imam and his smooth and cunning words. I sat there thinking to myself, "So, now I know how Adam and Eve felt when the Serpent kept badgering them with, "Hath God really said this?"

We all decided enough was enough—interesting how all of us, about a dozen or so, just happened to get to the same decision at the very same second, "Time to go. We've all heard enough."

I knew all of us were wondering, "How do we get out of this clever rut of, "We all worship the same God insanity."

I prayed—I'd been praying for the last 60 minutes or so for help. I knew I was no match for this clever leader of all the North American Muslim, terrorist community. I prayed for God to give me insight.

We left the Mosque and walked out the gate to stand on the public sidewalk and with police protection to hand out Gospel tracts to the Muslims leaving the service.

I stood there at the gate large enough for 2 cars to drive through, dreading the several thousand Muslims who would file by and I knew they were briefed to tell us that we serve the same God. What would I say? How could I match this puzzle the imam created for us. I knew I couldn't. Just pray. Don't leave. Pass out the tracts.

The first Muslim man approached me, I handed him a tract—which he did not take. Instead he stopped and said, "Why are you here? Why the hate? Why do you hate us? We all serve the same God—so you are here with a message of hate."

I stood there praying, asking the Holy Spirit to give me words. How could I answer him after his Imam had done such a clever job that even the President of the United States, and the Secretary of State had bought this con job.

I just prayed. I prayed and when the Muslim man stopped and a crowd had gathered to see how I would respond; to watch me make a fool of myself … I began to say—"Jesus commanded us to take the Gospel to everyone and we are here to do this. But I didn't—I stopped before saying this and I do not know why, but I just began with, "Jesus is God."

The Muslim man drew back and stared at me. He drew himself up and said, "NO." This is THE Difference. NO. We do NOT worship the same God."

And that was the answer—"I looked at him and the prayers had been answered, "Jesus is God I repeated—and the other eleven men began to tell the Muslims before them, "Jesus is God." We all smiled—and we all just repeated over and over again, "Jesus is God."

God gave us the words to say—and the words were so simple, yet so profound that the con game ended immediately.

Jesus is God … that's all any Christian has to tell any Muslim when they ask the trip up statement, "We all worship the same God."

Jesus is God. That's all we have to say. Jesus does the rest. Steve Klein teaches others to respect the Law written on the heart, which was given by Jesus, who is God.

18

NOSE WIPERS

The word of the LORD came to me: "Son of man, prophesy against the shepherds of Israel" (Ezekial 34).

I love men of God, bold, unwavering, and unwilling to compromise. I know many. I especially love it when a Shepherd fits that mold. I love many of them and, believe it or not, many of them love me too.

A coach and pastor have kindred spirits. They both deal with people, exhort people to be more than they think they can be, and take the heat during bad times. A good Pastor/Coach is not afraid of criticism. Some of my greatest growth has occurred when a friend was honest with me. God bless the real shepherds. You are heroes! I hear from them often. Several encouraged me to write this piece.

But the hireling is a different story. He is more dangerous than the Devil because he gives the sheep a sense of security that does not exist. Sadly, hirelings fill many of our pulpits. It is to them that I write.

No wonder we are in the mess we are in. If you would have read some of the email that I received in response to Sheep Without Shepherds you would know what I mean. Where in the world did all of these hyper-sensitive pastors come from, anyway? What makes them immune to criticism?

I know I make other Christians nervous. I'm not always sure why that is, and to be honest with you, I wish everyone liked me. But, that's not the way things are and I've learned to live with that fact. As Frank Sinatra sang, "I Gotta Be Me."

"You are like the thing in the middle of the washing machine....the agitator..." Pastor Greg wrote. *"You slap us around real good, shake us all up, and send us off with our heads spinning. I haven't figured out yet if I like it or not, but I do have to admit you knock the starch out of us."*

If he thinks my writing is biting, I wonder if he has ever listened to my radio show Pass The Salt: Talk Radio With a Sting. Tune in for a listen, but

I warn you, it is salty…not sugary. Some like it, some don't; but even my detractors would have to admit that it adds a bit of spice to their mundane form of Churchianity. Check it out. It's free.

Many of the emails I received were from some of the why-are-you-so harsh pastors, *"If you knew how hard our job was…yada yada, yada."* I'm not sure what they mean by hard. It certainly isn't manually challenging—although constantly side-stepping the Truth might make one nimble on his feet! I assume they mean the people-pleasing part of the job is challenging. Wiping noses does tend to wear one out.

But I don't feel sorry for them. For many people, life is hard, not just for pastors, and it seems to me that things would be a lot easier on everyone if the Shepherd taught the sheep how to fend for themselves rather than wiping the sheeps' nose as he tells them how brave they are. I know, I know, I am so judgmental.

Disclaimer: I used to tell my football players, *"If I ever call you a bunch of sissies, don't take it personally…unless you are a sissy. If you are a sissy, listen extra closely."* (I'm not speaking to every pastor, but if the shoe fits…)

Don't forget, I spent a long career as a coach. Every decision I made was second-guessed by somebody. It is the nature of the job. I never went home and whined to my wife and kids about how hard the job was, or how harsh the fans were, or that no one appreciated me. The scoreboard didn't lie. Nobody cared how hard my job was -- they just expected us to win. I forged the boys into men. I decided if someone was going to be upset with my decisions it would be them, not me. I found that you sleep a lot better when you stand up for what you believe.

Strange isn't it? The Devil and his acolytes aren't trying to be liked, they're playing to win. Our team cowers in the corner in the face of criticism and whines. If you can't take the heat get another line of work.

"Go suck your thumb," I found myself telling more than one of the pew-sitters (fans). *"I'd love to see your job performance judged live by 4,000 people every Friday night. Leading men ain't no job for wimps. My job requires that the players perform and unfortunately too many of the players act like their mom and dad. I don't have time for thumb-suckers."* (I got a little nicer after I was saved.)

So, how is your team doing Pastor? Are you committed to fighting for Truth or are you trying to be nicer than Jesus. At least he upset some tables in the church I might add.

Tired of the stress? Tell the sheep to grow up. It's Scriptural, you know? Sorry, I have no sympathy for men who want to wipe noses for a living. You won't be nearly as stressed if you fight over Truth rather than over the color of the carpet in the sanctuary. The enemies of Christianity are training their sons to be warriors while Christians teach our sons how to get in touch with their feelings. They are learning to cut our throat as we learn to turn our cheek.

Look folks, God is a man. Sorry if this doesn't fit your emerging theology but God is the Father, NOT our mother. He is masculine. (My dad can beat up your dad!)

Whatever happened to men in the pulpits? Where did we get this current batch of nurses? (Now, now…if the shoe fits…) *"Oh, Coach you are so mean."*

Here is what I don't get. Where did it become off limits to challenge a pastor? Oh, I know the Scripture "Saying, Touch not mine anointed," but that begs a different question. How do we know who is anointed and who is not? I promise you there are many pastors who are not anointed of God. Jesus called them hirelings, those who are just in it for the paycheck.

I think it is time we called them out. What if I told them I was anointed to rebuke them? Presumptuous, you might say, or a bit arrogant? Maybe so! But I'm just a fan in the bleachers watching a lousy performance and pointing my fingers at the coach. Seems to me the one's who want to criticize me are the same ones who allowed this mess to develop. They probably criticize the football coach on Friday nights at their local high school game.

So, I wrote a commentary challenging the "shepherds" and you would have thought I committed blasphemy. Where do these guys get off? Darkness is swallowing up this nation and the "shepherds" get mad at me because I spoke some "harsh" words about their performance. Put your armor on, Brother, there is a war a-raging for the souls of men. You are supposed to be on the front lines. Suck it up!

They'd never make it as a football coach.

One of those pompous fellows sent me an email telling me that *"It is fanatics like you that give Christians a bad name."* (I fought off the urge to say *"go suck your thumb, you Pharisee."*) But he nailed the problem. Too many shepherds ARE more worried about how Christians LOOK rather than defending the Truth. Jesus didn't operate on polls and He was called the Rock of Offense for thumb-sucking sakes! The folks IN THE CHURCH killed him!

I only wish they fought evil as much as they fought me.

During my coaching career I saw many a player wilt under the pressure of the battle. Never once did we run into the huddle and apologize to them for pushing them so hard. When they felt like quitting we reminded them what they were fighting for, we <u>challenged their manhood</u>, encouraged them to fight. *No crying in baseball!*

So now I have hurt the feelings of some pastors. I didn't give them the honor they deserve. Says who? Honor isn't given, honor is earned. Leadership is an activity, not a position. Paul didn't say to give honor to everyone. He said *"<u>Render therefore to all their dues: tribute to whom tribute is due; custom to whom custom; fear to whom fear; honour to whom honour.</u>* Maybe if some of them rendered fear to the Lord they would be more deserving of honor. It seems to me that Paul made honor conditional.

Buck up, Pastor. Tighten your belt and earn your meal money. You are a servant of the Lord, a General in the Army of God, God's ambassador here on the earth. Get your thumb out of your mouth and pick up a few stones.

To quote William Wallace, Scottish freedom fighter: *There's a difference between us. You think the people of this country exist to provide you with position. I think your position exists to provide those people with freedom. And I go to make sure that they have it.*

Vince Lombardi said, *"Coaches who can outline plays on a blackboard are a dime a dozen. The ones who win get inside their player and motivate.* <u>The Apostle Paul said it this way.</u> *"For as the body without the spirit is dead, so faith without works is dead also."*

We need you, Pastor, more than you will ever know. You are not getting the job done. Getting mad over what I write does not change that fact. Your team is un-prepared for the battle.

I agree with Charles Finney: If there is a decay of conscience, the pulpit is responsible for it. If the public press lacks moral discernment, the pulpit is responsible for it. If the church is degenerate and worldly, the pulpit is responsible for it. If the world loses its interest in Christianity, the pulpit is responsible for it. If Satan rules in our halls of legislation, the pulpit is responsible for it. If our politics become so corrupt that the very foundations of our government are ready to fall away, the pulpit is responsible for it." Maybe he didn't know how hard the job of a pastor was. <u>Have I therefore become your enemy because I tell you the truth?</u>

Get your thumb out of your mouth. Lead, follow, or get out of the pulpit. In HIS Service, Coach

"If the foundations be destroyed, what can the righteous do?"

Author's note: The hope and love of Jesus is so deep, speaking to us about our eternity. Jesus wishes that none would perish, but sadly looks on as those that claim His name do not bear the fruit of the Spirit (Galatians 5:22,23). There are many false converts, and some in that number stand behind many of the pulpits. Where was the church leadership, while evil has been working to destroy the foundations. A reminder, Hitler stated he knew that he could destroy the Church at will, because of greed, pride, and fear. Would then, many in church leadership be considered as traitors and sinners by their actions or inactions? Judgment indeed must begin in the House of God. Shepherds, where are you in the battle, are you a good talker, or do you follow Christ into action in the weightier issues of the day?

19

WHAT HAVE YOU DONE?

Once again our efforts on the streets were shunned by the institutionalized church. Believe it or not, Las Vegas is a city replete with "church buildings." Several mega mall-like churches battle the casinos for customers, content to live in comfort with the sin, and unwilling to go "all in" in an attempt to "run the table" over decadence. They are fearful of driving folks away to another venue where they can "ante up" and join the religious game. The "churches" don't get it. Try as we might we have not been successful at convincing them that the battle for the souls of men lies on the streets of Las Vegas.

Standing in a pulpit and speaking against sin is not the same as confronting sin. To apply a little Shakespeare to those hiding behind the pulpit, preaching about sin is being full of "sound and fury, signifying nothing." It is the same as a newsman reporting on a war and somehow thinking he was part of it. It is like a liberal who speaks against global warming as he travels the nation on a private jet. To paraphrase Paul, "speech without corresponding action, is dead."

One pastor, who at least had the courage to host our nightly worship services, explained to us that his church shared a property line with an abortion clinic. Now let that sink in....this church had an abortion clinic as a next-door neighbor...yet the clinic continued to thrive in its baby-slaughter business. The pastor told us that every service he had the congregation "stand, lift their hands towards the clinic, and pray that the evil would cease." (I'm not making this up.) I wonder if Jesus would have been so cavalier towards a life-destroying ministry that He shared a fence post with? Although the pastor opened his church to us, he did not adjure his "sheep" to join us.

It happens every where we go. They let us use the building but do nothing to help us fill it. They are afraid of the Truth that their sheep might hear. But it gets worse. The pastor at the largest church/Christian mall in Vegas told his flock to "have nothing to do" with us. (Let that sink in too.....have nothing to do with fellow Christians...and I'm sure they are known throughout the community for "their love.") They just don't love Truth, or their neighbors, enough to share the Truth with them. But, the church is growing (as are the number of casinos...and there are SIX abortuaries in town) so the Lord is "blessing their ministry" with more butts and bucks.

But it is what it is.... So, you may ask, what does this have to do with you? You are the one who chooses the shepherd under whom you sit. Explaining to our Lord that you followed the advice on a poor Shepherd from some Christian CEO or Bishop will not hold much sway in Heaven's Hall's of Justice. Although works are not necessary for salvation, the Apostle Paul makes it very clear that works are the fruits of salvation. Do you have any fruit? I'm talking about you. Not your church, not your pastor. YOU! Pray for them and help them become a real MAN of God, take them into the actions.

On the awesome moment when you stand before Him and cast your crown at His feet, will there be any jewels in your crown? Listen folks, the arrival of Jesus Christ into the earth realm transformed the Faith of our Fathers from a religion to a personal relationship. No longer do you access The Christ through Rabbis, Priests, and Pastors, but through the Spirit of the Living God given on the Day of Pentecost. He lives in you. It is to Him that you will give account. With that in mind, let me ask a question that is intended to pierce your conscience. Some may call it harsh, some will complain that I am too direct, but I pray that this question will serve as a floodlight into your heart. What have YOU done?

Don't tell me you have prayed. Praying is not doing. In the Garden Jesus prayed...but He got up and went. Where would man be today if Jesus had not been spurred to action? What if he had never gotten off of His knees? What if he had counted on others to do the dirty work? For God so loved the world that HE DID SOMETHING....what about you?

I ask you again...what have you DONE?

- About the slaughter of 50 million little baby boys and girls.

- About the pornography gushing down the streets of our cities.

- About the homosexual indoctrination of children in your government school.

- About the laissez faire attitude towards divorce in the church.

- About the spiritual abuse doled out by church leadership in some "churches." What have you done?

- About the legal terrorism directed at those who publicly proclaim Christ.

- About the promotion of "self-help" books over the Bible in your "church."

- About the transformation of the Constitution to nothing more than toilet paper.

- About the lies of humanism superseding the Truth of the Scriptures.

- About the perpetuation of war in the name of peace.

- About the loss of liberty in the pursuit of comfort. WHAT have you done?

The Scriptures teach us that one day we will all stand before the Lord and give an account for the deeds we have done in the flesh. That we will be responsible for things we have done, and things we have left undone. It is our ACTIONS that will be on trial; Not our thoughts, not our wishes, and not our intentions. *"Therefore to him that knoweth to do good, and doeth it not, to him it is sin"* (James 4:17).

When was the last time your church Shepherd told you that? If I understand the concept correctly, the jewels in your crown represent the souls you brought to the Lord, the things you did for the sake of the Gospel. What a shame to stand before the Lord with only a dime-store tiara to cast at His feet. So tell me....what have you done? Coach

20

PORNOGRAPHY IS DANGEROUS

*ASK RAPISTS AND CHILD MOSLESTERS, BUT WHAT ABOUT ASKING SHEPHERDS?

Lord, heal and give grace to your Shepherds to come back to you, strengthen them. After running for Governor of Missouri, I wanted to first thank God and all those who supported me, but mostly for the Christian brothers and sisters that were searching for His Truth. Much work still needs to be done to return the sovereignty of this country back to its proper order of God, family, and nation (to give our posterity the greatest opportunity for freedom in the future as part of a Constitutional Republic under God).

With that being said, there is indeed much work that needs to be done to protect our children and families from many directions. Why aren't Shepherds standing in front of places like video stores to bring awareness that some places help bring pornography into the homes and are putting children and families at great risk. Why aren't they telling their people weekly not to shop at these places that support Satan's perversions.

More than 65 studies have shown that dangerous offenders (child molesters, killers, and rapists) often use porn before becoming offenders and use it during illegal acts, according to the American Life League. (They are not only more likely to commit their crimes if they employ pornography; they are likely to precede their violent acts with extended use of deviant materials. Male sex offenders soon begin to display addictive and compulsive behavior when using porn. Their mechanisms for relieving stress soon all become related to deviant sex. They offend more and more often). The league says that about 2 million pedophiles, rapists, child molesters, sadists, and those who solicit teenage or child prostitutes commit more than 2 million crimes annually. This number accounts only for those incidents that are reported; the total number is obviously much higher.

Those naive individuals who cling to the quaint and outmoded belief that pornography is "victimless" should wake up and look at the facts. (Thousands of persons have been tortured, raped, and murdered by warped human beings as a direct result of pornography. There are thousands of such cases cramming police files all over the Nation). My question to you is this: is it possible that Family & Video or other video stores with their pornography in the back room, has indirectly given aid and comfort to a rapist or child molester of your area? Is it possible that people that rent at Family video and other such stores unknowingly help it be possible?

Is it possible that the church in your area are like some of the good parents and grandparents that we've talked to at Family & Video and unaware of the perversions in the back room of Family & Video and other such stores? Is it possible that now the church Shepherds are aware that this Family & Video and some other stores are putting members in their congregation's families and their neighbors at risk now and for eternity, will go out and stand, and ask that members not support this destruction of families in any way? (I invite the Shepherds, church members and concerned citizens to stand up and lets start taking back our communities from those that directly or indirectly , through their actions or inactions, are enemies of the virtues of our children and families and putting them at risk both now and eternally).

I also invite the mayors, city council members, school teachers and administrators, legislators and others in leadership that say they are concerned about the children and their families to stand with us, or step down from their jobs. These pretend family places have no First Amendment right to censor the virtues of the children and bring perversion into the families, and they lie to the people to say this is so. Please do something, as this is happening because of the pulpits.

21

WHY GRAPHIC SIGNS?
SHEPHERDS PLEASE STOP THE SLAUGHTER.

Words have failed and we need to see the horrible reality of what we are doing to the weakest among us in our nation. The pictures we carry provide a pictorial essay and a real warning of what horrors befall a culture that turns its back on a Holy God. Our children need to know that the choices they make and the actions they take have lasting consequences. Life and blessing are ours when we honor the Ten Commandments found in God's law. This is visibly demonstrated by the picture of a live baby. Contrast this with the graphic pictures of children ripped apart by abortion, and you epitomize the cost of walking away from the precepts and principles found in God's law.

"This day I call heaven and earth as witnesses against you that I have set before you life and death, blessings and curses. Now choose life, so that you and your children may live..." (Deuteronomy 30:19).

Do These Pictures Traumatize Children?

No! They traumatize adults attempting to deny the truth and the horror of abortion! That's right! These pictures do not traumatize our kids, no matter how young they are. Children are not traumatized if they have parents who teach that abortion is a terrible thing to do to a child. Our children who have grown up in this ministry know that this is a picture of a baby who is hurt. They also know that their mom and dad are doing everything they can to help these voiceless children.

It is the parents who tell their children that abortion is a good thing, or a "mother's choice," that have difficulty explaining the graphic pictures to their children. They are terrorized and traumatized because they have no words to justify what their children have seen. The kids are left wondering if mom and dad would "choose" to do the same thing to them.

"Do not hate your brother in your heart. Rebuke your neighbor frankly so you will not share in his guilt" (Leviticus 19:17).

Is This Terrorism?

No! The truth brings terror only to the one who is doing wrong. He fears being exposed. In order to avoid the horrible truth that these pictures uncover, the enemy attempts to point his finger at someone else—us! When one loses an argument, he resorts to argument "ad hominem" (name calling). Planned Parenthood and its ilk seek to paint all Christians who are telling the truth and living out their faith in the public forum as "wild eyed, fundamentalist, lunatic, terrorists."

"Have I now become your enemy by telling you the truth" (Galatians 4:23)?

Is This Extreme?

No, graphic pictures are not extreme! This is what parents do when they feel their children are in danger. The horrible pictures of traffic accidents used prolifically in driver's education courses are not viewed as extreme. They teach what words cannot. The pictures of Jews stacked like cords of wood outside Nazi concentration camps are not considered extreme when depicting the murderous truth of Nazism. It should never be considered extreme when one tries to rescue children from a treacherous lie by pictorially telling the truth. We will make no attempt to appear fair and open-minded to the lies and "coverups" of the abortion industry. We desire only to be true to the Gospel of Jesus Christ. In so doing we believe that God Himself will give our kids eyes to see the real horror of abortion.

"Have nothing to do with the fruitless deeds of darkness, but rather expose them" (Ephesians 5:11).

What Would Jesus Do?

Would Jesus carry graphic pictures? He already has. That's right! When words fail, God speaks to us in living parables (pictures). Jesus was and is God's most graphic picture of His magnificent love toward us. Jesus became a living parable of the high cost and degrading horror of our sin. It cost Him His life. He was publicly humiliated and hung naked on a cross. He was wounded and bruised. He bled and He died. He was marred beyond even looking like a man.

Jesus was and is God's graphic picture of His love toward us.

Jesus' sacrificial and graphic death on a cross helps us to understand the magnitude of God's love. It was an ugly death. It was and still is repugnant to our senses. It was and still is disturbing. It creates within our hearts a conflict that we would just as soon ignore. But, because He loves us, He drew a picture of His love with His Son's death on an old rugged cross. He has afflicted us, and has brought conflict to us with this graphic truth, not because He hates us, but because He loves us!

"But God demonstrated His own love for us in this: While we were still sinners, Christ died for us" (Romans 5:8).

The Entire Sacrificial System Points to God's Graphic Ways!

Sacrifice in the Old Testament was an ugly business. It was acceptable only on the basis of very graphic procedures. God used the sacrificial system as a graphic pedagogical device to teach His people the severity of sin. "Without the shedding of blood there is no remission of sins." Can you imagine laying your hand on the head of a precious lamb and slitting its throat with the other?

Can you imagine watching the crimson blood flow as the animal dies in your hands? The flowing red blood was a graphic teacher of the severity of sin. It prepared those in Old Testament times for the coming of the final sacrifice, the lamb of God, Jesus Christ.

Now, just imagine bringing your eight-year-old son with you and explaining to him why a lamb must die for the forgiveness of that boy's sins. Imagine that this was a family lamb that had been raised for this very purpose. The son was witness to a very graphic truth which prepared him to be a man. A young man, who is raised to understand the severity of his own sin and the high price paid that he might be forgiven, is one who is ready to be a man.

Should We Carry Such Graphic Pictures?

Yes, we must. God is calling us to expose the lies that are covering up the slaughter of innocent human beings. Place the picture of a live baby next to the picture of a baby ripped apart by abortion and ask, "Which one do you choose?"

You will find that kids, almost 100% of the time, will choose the picture of the live baby. Do the same thing with adults and you will find that those who are "prochoice" simply shut their mouths. They have nothing to say. All of their logic breaks down when they are faced with the graphic truth.

In the prophet Jeremiah's time, the people of Israel were also sacrificing their children in the valley of Ben Hinnom. God said that this was "...something I did not command, nor did it ever enter my mind" (Jeremiah 7:31).

God Himself was astonished at the depravity of His children, sacrificing their own sons and daughters to false gods. Could this be America today? The problem was that the people of God in Jeremiah's time did not, "...plead the case of the fatherless towin it..."(Jeremiah 5:28).

Today, we in the Church of Jesus Christ are not pleading the case of the fatherless to win it. Oh, we build our crisis pregnancy centers, vote Republican, participate in Life Chain, and preach our annual Roe v. Wade sermon on January 22. We are not, however, pleading the case of the over 45 million children murdered and those soon to be killed, so as to win it.

As for me and my house, we have determined to plead the case of the fatherless to win it. Graphic pictures expose the devil's schemes and make the defense of the "pro-choice" lie, indefensible. Flip Benham Director OSA

22

BLACK REGIMENT

"If there is a decay of conscience, the pulpit is responsible for it. If the public press lacks moral discernment, the pulpit is responsible for it. If the church is denigrate and worldly, the pulpit is responsible for it. If the world loses its interest in Christianity, the pulpit is responsible for it. If Satan rules in our halls of legislation, the pulpit is responsible for it. If our politics become so corrupt that the very foundations of our government are ready to fall, the pulpit is responsible for it."
—*Rev. Charles Finney*

Why does it seem that Americans are the only people on earth who are blind to the truth and ignorant of their own history? Wherever you look, we can see the vision of freedom that once deluged our shores being swept away. We have to wonder how much longer our American Republic can survive.

Our government has become the great candy machine spewing out an endless stream of treats to lucky people, and we have to pay the bill for it. I am talking about trillions of hard earned wages every single year and the government's appetite just keeps growing, getting bigger and bigger and bigger.

What we need in this nation of ours is a political revolution, just like the one we had in 1776. Above all, I believe we need pastors and other Christian leaders who are willing to stand up to our current batch of spoiled secular bureaucrats who read and understand such great patriots as Noah Webster, who in his History of the United States wrote:

"Almost all the civil liberty now enjoyed in the world owes its origin to the principles of the Christian religion......The religion which has introduced civil liberty is the religion of Christ and His apostles, which enjoins humility, piety, and benevolence; which acknowledges in every person a brother or sister and a citizen with equal rights. This is genuine Christianity and to this we owe our free constitution of government."

We need Shepherds who reject the lie that our national ideals stem from the influence of the French Enlightenment rather than from the Bible and Christianity, pastors who, with John Wingate Thornton, understand that *"To the Pulpit, we owe the moral force which won our independence."* We need pastors who realize that our independence today stems from one thing and one thing only: from the biblical concept that all men are created in the image of God, and because of this all men are entitled to equal treatment and *unalienable rights.*

In short, we need Shepherds who are willing to join today's "Black Regiment." The Black Regiment was a group of clergy who were fierce opponents of British tyranny and a driving force in the decision of the colonies to seek independence. King George had provoked many of these men to leave England by demanding that they submit to licensing by the crown. He called them the Black Regiment because of the black robes they wore when preaching.

These men of God staunchly opposed the divine right of kings. Their cry was, "No King but King Jesus." Many of them wrote impassioned pleas for freedom, and some even joined the Continental Army. When George Washington asked Lutheran Pastor John Muhlenberg to raise a regiment of volunteers, Muhlenberg gladly agreed. Before marching off to join Washington's army, he delivered a powerful sermon from Ecclesiastes 3:1-8 that concluded with these words: "The Bible tells us there is a time for all things and there is a time to preach and a time to pray, but the time for me to preach has passed away, and there is a time to fight, and that time has come now. Now is the time to fight! Call for recruits! Sound the drums." Then Muhlenberg took off his clerical robe to reveal the uniform of a Virginia Colonel. Grabbing his musket from behind the pulpit, he donned his Colonel's hat and marched off to war.

Patriotic Christian friend of mine, are you willing to say, "I will fight for the truth. I will be beholden to no one (whether a Democrat, Republican or Other) except Jesus Christ. I will stand up to those seeking to enslave us all by sending our children to their deaths as they build their New World Order and as they tax us into poverty. I will seek to bind our politicians with the chains of the Constitution. And I will do this for the glory of God and the advancement of Christian liberty?" And yes, the dues will be high (radical obedience), but your treasure in heaven will more than amply repay. May God grant you boldness to join the battle!

Pastor Mark Kiser

23

TAKE THE MUZZLE OFF

It's about time!
Finally a little bit of offense out of the good guys. I have been so frustrated over the past years as I watch our "team" continue to run our defensive unit out onto the field.

It is not the job of the defense to score points. It is their job to prevent the other team from scoring. For as long as I have been engaged in the cultural war it has been a rare sight to see our guys "throw a punch." The rope-a-dope may have worked for Muhammad Ali but that strategy has done nothing to help the cause of Christianity in today's America.

Our opponents have used the judicial ropes to tie up the Christian dopes. But finally, our guys are about to take a swing.

As I have written many times, it is my belief that the paralyzing lie of "separation between the church and state" has done more to restrict Christianity than anything in my life-time.

We are in trouble in America <u>because the pulpits have gone silent</u>. There are several different reason why this has happened but the greatest lie has been that one's religion has no place in politics. For most of us, <u>our religion frames our worldview</u>, the way we see the events around us, and because of the tyrannical courts and their miss application of the First Amendment, Christians have been forced to keep their views locked up inside their "stained glass fortresses." (Where Are Our Shepherds?)

Haven't you noticed that there are all kinds of religions welcome in America today: Paganism, Atheism, Environmentalism, Darwinism and a myriad of others have free reign inside our government schools. Christianity, which gave us the idea of "freedom of religion," is now the one on the outside looking in.

How has this happened? The courts have stuck a big sock in the mouth of our pulpits. As a result evil has run almost unopposed in our culture with a devastating effect on all facets of society. Christian values under gird the foundations of this once-great nation. Founding Father <u>Jedediah Morse</u> said:

"To the kindly influence of Christianity we owe that degree of civil freedom, and political and social happiness which mankind now enjoys. . . . Whenever the pillars of Christianity shall be overthrown, our present republican forms of government, and all blessings which flow from them, must fall with them."

"If the foundations be destroyed what can the righteous do" (Psalm 11:3)?

Let me clear one thing up. I have been screaming for years that we are <u>fighting the wrong battle</u>. We constantly find ourselves groveling at the table of government begging for our "constitutional rights." To quote from what I wrote over two years ago:

"I don't mean to be rude, but I think it is important to point out that we are fighting on the wrong field. With all due respect, the church does not receive her rights from the benevolence of the government. The 1st Amendment of the Constitution says 'Congress shall make no law regarding the establishment of a religion, nor prohibiting the free exercise thereof.' The 501-c3 statute limits the free exercise of the church by curbing her free-speech rights. The law, which was passed by congress, is a clear violation of the free exercise clause of the Constitution and according to the US Supreme Court in Marbury v Madison 'all laws repugnant to the Constitution are null and void.' The right of churches and church leaders to freely speak <u>comes from God and not from the government</u>. The Declaration of Independence states 'that to secure these rights governments are instituted amongst men, deriving their just powers from the consent of the governed.' The Church is above, not separate, from the government. We are fighting on the wrong field." Congress shall make no law—and neither can the courts.

Look, I know all about the trap that the government has set in regards to the 501 (c) 3 restrictions on churches that become corporations. To incorporate a church is to come into relationship with the government that God never intended the church to enter. Incorporation makes the government the CEO of the church. It makes Caesar the boss of the incorporated church. Churches should not incorporate. Most do it out of ignorance and by doing so they insert their own sock into the pastor's mouth. Afraid to lose their tax-exemption the church slowly begins to answer to Caesar rather than to God. No man can serve two masters.

You see, churches are tax <u>IMMUNE</u>, or protected from government, and not tax <u>EXEMPT</u> which means "free from obligation." The church has no obligation to government…until they incorporate. Once they do, they make a deal with the Devil. They now answer to Caesar. That is the law. I say it is about time we fight back! Can someone tell me why the only "religion" that has a muzzle on its spokesmen is Christianity? Atheists are free to speak. So are Humanists, Union Leaders, Jesse Jackson, Al Sharpton, and Darwinists. Why are pastors and church leaders the only ones banished from the public square? They are scared by the non-existent "separation between the church and state" and the henchmen at the IRS. Thank God for the ADF and their willingness to pick a fight. "…in 1954 with the passage of the "Johnson amendment" which restricted the right of churches and pastors to speak Scriptural truth about candidates for office. The Johnson amendment was proposed by then-Senator Lyndon Johnson, and it changed the Internal Revenue Code to prohibit churches and other non-profit organizations from supporting or opposing a candidate for office. After the Johnson amendment passed, churches faced a choice of either continuing their tradition of speaking out or silencing themselves in order to retain their church's tax exemption. The Internal Revenue Service, in conjunction with radical organizations like Americans United for Separation of Church and State, have used the Johnson amendment to create an atmosphere of intimidation and fear for any church that dares to speak Scriptural truth about candidates for office or issues.

It is time for the intimidation and threats to end. Churches and pastors have a constitutional right to speak freely and truthfully from the pulpit—even on candidates and voting—without fearing loss of their tax exemption. Freedom of speech and freedom of religion are God-given rights, they are not Constitutional rights. Only God grants rights. The Constitution restricts government intrusion into our lives. It is time to cut the head off of that giant. Here is what I really like about it. It is going to expose a lot of pastors who have been hiding behind the so-called government restriction on free speech. With that barrier removed maybe we can more clearly distinguish between the brave men who speak for God and those who just love the cushy job. Interested in picking a fight? You'll find all of the information you need at http://www.alliancedefensefund.org/issues/religiousfreedom/churchandstate.aspx?cid=4491. The ADF has a game-plan. All they need is a few good men! Come on Pastor! Get off of the ropes!

Authors note: Understand that the ADF also has Satan within its system, pray for these men, that they are able to stand with no compromise, their talents could increase if they would first look to Jesus and know that any gift that they have is by the grace of God and not their own, strengthen their resolve to do what is right in God's eyes with no rationalization that they know best. Something you need to embed in your being as well as the Shepherds, listen up. *"Trust in the LORD with all your heart, And lean not on your own understanding; In all your ways acknowledge Him, And He shall direct your path"* (Proverbs 3:5,6).

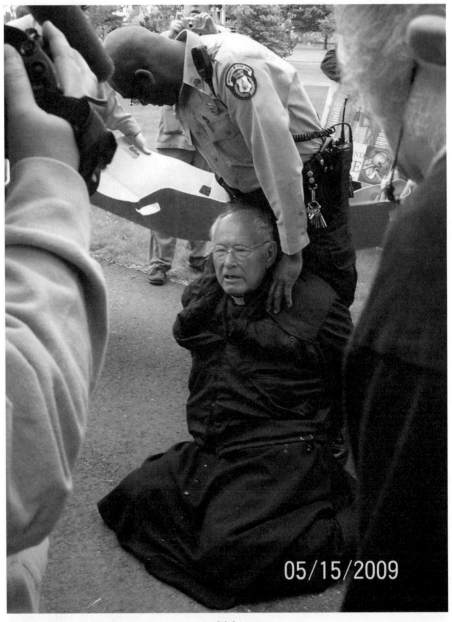

05/15/2009

24

LIGHT A FIRE UNDER
YOUR PASTOR

Here is a stern warning to pastors. Write it off if you like. The folks in the pew are greatly dissatisfied. I hear it when I speak in churches and I hear it every time I write a commentary. George Barna tells us that churches are hemorrhaging members and sadly, the leadership wants to blame the sheep. A good coach never blames the players. The sheep are a reflection of the shepherd. Read Hosea 4:6-8.

Pastors are coaches. They deal with people. Most successful coaches have a very firm set of fundamentals by which they operate. They are not running a popularity contest, they are leading a team. The best way to get your butt beat is to compromise on what you believe.

MANY have emailed me asking, *"What should we do, Coach? Our pastor won't preach the hard truth anymore. It is all the "feel-good" stuff. We are dying of starvation."*

I am often accused of pointing out problems but rarely offering solutions. Well, you asked for it, so I will tell you what I think.

This is risky because the "Church of the Status Quo" and her apostles are sure to attack you. They will accuse you of "criticizing the local church" and "church bashing." But you should love them enough to tell them the Truth. President Lincoln said, *"I do the best I know how; the very best I can; and I mean to keep doing so until the end. If the end brings us out wrong ten thousand angels swearing I was right will not make any difference."*

Paul said it this way, *"Am I therefore become your enemy, because I tell you the truth?"*

My dad was a great guy, but little things used to drive him crazy. One of the things that used to bug him the most was when he would come home from the factory in the winter and the fire in the fireplace was barely burning. He would grab the poker and turn to one of us and say,

"How many times do I have to tell you that you can't lay a big log on top of the

fire or you will smother it? A big log will only burn if there is a good base of hot coals burning underneath. You can't start a fire with a big log."

So here is the analogy. (I'm sure my dad never dreamed his words would go around the world.)

The pastor is the log and those sitting in the pews are the kindling…the little wood that sets the big log on fire. For too long we have tried to convince the big log that he needed to catch on fire. Every time a spark was lit he would roll over and smother the flame. "Wild fire" is one thing the big logs hate. The big logs want "natural-gas" fires that they can control the flame on.

"It does not require a majority to prevail, but rather an irate, tireless minority keen to set brush fires in people's minds." --Samuel Adams.

Okay, Mr. Kindling-Wood, you have a decision you are going to have to make. Are you sick and tired enough to come out of your comfort zone and begin to set little brush-fires? If you are not willing to make a stand then you have no reason to complain. It is time to stop waiting on the big log to set the rest of you on fire. As my friend Pete, once said, "Our leaders will never see the light until we turn up the heat."

Here are a few things to do to change the temperature in your church. (Warning: You will be called all kinds of names by your "brothers in Christ." They will say you are "sowing discord amongst the brethren….that you shouldn't bring politics into the church, and the worse name of all, "a resister."

You're not sowing discord. You are asking questions. It is a church body…. not a monarchy. Pastors deserve your respect, not blind allegiance. (Author's note: you are both to be part of the body, so pray together, and for each other, and expect the best from each other as it relates to those things we have been taught by Christ.)

1. Stop calling your elected officials and start calling your pastor. Every time you see something that your local church should be concerned about, call your pastor and ask him a very simple question: "Pastor, what is our church going to do about it?" His response will tell you a lot about him. Do it privately at first as the Scriptures teach.

2. Don't let him "wiggle off of the hook." Follow up in a day or two and see if he has progressed in his plan to oppose evil. Let him know that you have shared your concern with others in the congregation and that they are waiting to hear his response as well.

3. Tell him you have decided to go to the school board (as an example of an issue that you might have brought to him) and ask him if he will go with you.

4. Continue to email and hard copy him on information germane to the topic. Be persistent. Don't let him say later that "he didn't know."

5. After a hard sermon, make sure that you let him know that you appreciate what he had to say. Then ask this, "Pastor, what can I do to help you fight this in our community?" (Be careful, he may start quaking but let him know you are serious.)

6. Note: You are creating a sense of accountability here. Demand in the name of Christ, that he walk the walk and not just talk the talk. Let him know you are expecting his leadership, as are others.

7. If he rarely preaches a hard sermon, ask, "Pastor, I haven't heard a sermon on the sins of abortion, homosexuality, and pornography recently, but do you have one planned?" Let him know it is important to you and continue to bring it up. Write notes to him.

8. Ask him who he is voting for in the next election and why. If he is voting for a pro-abort, or homo-sympathizer point it out to him. If he says he doesn't think he should share his personal political beliefs, please ask him why. It may be that he doesn't want to discuss it at church or in front of others, so take him out to lunch and "pin him down." Ask him if his personal beliefs are different from those he preaches. It is important to know what he believes.   Pray for him.

9. Get your hands on CDs, DVDs, and books and begin to educate YOURSELF on what is going on. Be like the <u>Bereans</u> who checked things out for themselves.   Pray for the Shepherds, and yourself that you or they would not be deceived.

10. Start a Bible Study in your home with like-minded folks. Ask the leadership to support it. You would think they would encourage the "assembling together of the saints" but usually, that means only where they can have you in a controlled environment. Leading a Bible Study will stretch you and make you more equipped to share your faith with others. This is a good thing. But, be warned that <u>the pastor may try to turn it into a controlled "small group"</u> that is more about building horizontal relationships among each other rather than a vertical relationship with God.

11. Withhold your tithe if he refuses to preach against sin—he may say something like, "I don't want to offend so-and-so." Tell your pastor that you are going to give your tithe money to a ministry that is preaching "<u>the whole-counsel of God</u>." Follow the Biblical edict to "<u>sow into good soil</u>." Many active ministries could use the help.

12. If he doesn't encourage his flock to carry Bibles to church, please ask him why. It may be that he wants to use several versions (possibly up on a screen) that can cause confusion. For example, Rick Warren, in his Purpose Driven book, selected verses from different versions to fit the scenario he needed to create. (A danger in not bringing your Bibles is that if the people in the pews cannot follow along, a pastor may someday introduce a New Age teaching that sounds biblical but few will catch it if they can't verify what he is teaching.)

13. Offer to start a "community watch-dog" ministry in the church to keep an eye on issues affecting Christians. Ask for his endorsement.

14. Offer to start a co-op for home educators and ask if the church would support you. If your pastor doesn't want to "offend the government school teachers" in his flock, then that is a red flag.

15. Ask him if Christians should vote for local school levies and why? Begin to share information about the dangers of public schools. (www. exodusmandate.org is a great place to start.)

16. Be prepared to leave your church. The answers that you get may not satisfy you. For the sake of your soul and the souls of your family find a church that is walking in the Truth.

It is time to turn up the heat. Those big logs will never burn until the kindling starts to glow red. Jesus warned us: "*So then because thou art lukewarm, and neither cold nor hot, I will spue thee out of my mouth.*" Accountability is a powerful tool.

Stop complaining about the lukewarm preaching. Put up or shut up. Light a fire and watch it spread. The big log will either catch your fire or roll on down the road! Snap, crackle, and pop. Dad would be proud of you.

25

ACT...CONTEND!

"With my whole heart have I sought thee: O let me not wander from your commandments. Your Word have I hid in mine heart, that I might not sin against thee (Psalm 119:10,11).

With all of the terrible things happening in Government, Hollywood, education, and many pulpits, remember that we have hope in Christ. He is not dead, He is our Living Savior.

His children are given a special wisdom as part of their faith that allows a joy in their risen Savior. His children are also given knowledge and understanding of the urgency of the times we live in, where the moral decay puts at risk the souls of millions of people in our once great country, with the greatest risk to our posterity. Fight, strive, contend for the faith. Now, more than ever, His children that hear His voice must be active in their witness, must do all they can, and when all is done, they must stand. Listen to the Word of God in Proverbs 4:18, *"But the path of the just is as the shining light, that shines more and more unto the perfect day."*

If we are to call Jesus, "Lord, Lord," then we are to have Him in charge of all parts of our lives and teach our children to love, honor and glorify Him. Can all of us see ourselves giving Him another stripe on His back as we allow others to educate our children in the atheistic environment of the government schools? These are schools that are run by those in government who are enemies of the people, and who are bringing down judgment upon the people as they stay silent.

Thank God that we have people around the country that are helping to wake up the sleeping Christians, as they take part in the Tea Parties, even as we must know that without Jesus it will fail. The taxes were mentioned as 17th on the list of grievances given to the King in the Declaration of Independence. Before taxes, they felt they were spurned with contempt at the foot of King George's throne because of the tyranny in the representative and judicial bodies. Today we have this contempt coming from all three branches of government. We recognize that there is no question that the times are growing darker because of this, and God's children know that it is happening because the Gospel is being challenged in this country like never before.

Judgment must indeed begin in the house of God. As our country deteriorates, the pulpits stay silent, curtailing their witness with an unproductive life. Many pastors may cry out with this sting, thinking with their people, that it is happening, but not in my church. We give to missions overseas, we give to the poor, we visit the sick and those in prison. These things we must not neglect, but we must be strong enough to say to our people, "

- RUN as fast as you can from the "Sacred Cow," the government schools.

- Meet me at the city council and we will shut down every place that sells pornography.

- Come with me to the abortion mills so that they murder no more, and we can save children, and mothers.

- Teach your children that homosexuality is a sin. Love the person but hate the sin, and let us go to the Government School Board meetings, stopping the lies that are taught to the children.

- Knowing that Islam is a lie from the pit of hell, pray for these lost souls, and we must actively let the legislature and schools know that all Islamic influence must be stopped in this country.

- Let's turn off our televisions for a month.

- Pray for me as a Shepherd that I do the will of God and put away the pride of my will.

These are but a few of the main issues facing the soul of this nation, and this advancing juggernaut is getting worse daily because the pulpits are silent, and His people are silent. As I say these things that we must address, because Jesus told us to have dominion and also to occupy until He returns, know that Jesus tells us in Scripture, *"If you can believe, all things are possible to him that believes. With men it is impossible, but not with God: for with God all things are possible"* (Mark 9:23, 10:27). Jesus gave us the greatest example of that when He rose from the dead. There is nothing greater than having power over death."

Smile, because even though things are getting worse daily, we are a friend of the ONE in control, and if you don't have a joy and peace beyond human understanding as we face tribulation, give us a call, because that should be a part of your faith in Jesus, who wants you to have no worry or fear of man. 417-894-5768

Act, Contend, Stand!!! Listen and let this guide you, as you remember that Jesus is not dead, HE is our living Savior.

26

THE TIME IS NOW!

"Woe to the shepherds who are destroying and scattering the sheep of my pasture!"
declares the LORD (Jeremiah 23:1).

It is again time for Christian patriots to protect their freedoms, declaring Independence from the anti-God, morally bankrupt, and corrupt Federal Government of the United States that is against the will of the people.

The Despotic Federal Government in the United States has betrayed the people and is not legitimate, causing more grievous injury to the people today, than was caused by the tyrants in England that precipitated the separation and signing of the original Declaration of Independence. The original Declaration of Independence would agree that whenever a government is against the laws of nature and nature's God, and against the Constitution put into place by the consent of the governed, that formed a Constitutional Republic under God, it becomes the right of the people to alter or abolish it. Let the real men and women that have eyes to see and ears to hear, understand that our future posterity will continue to be at greater risk until we separate from the Federal Government and any State Governments that have through traitorous acts, forfeited their right to govern the people.

Because we have turned our backs on the Biblical Foundations, traitors have become plentiful in all parts of our Government, and the despotism has become more aggressive and destructive to our families and our nation. A return to Christian principles that are protected by a Constitution, with the consent of the people that has declared dependence on God, is all that can save our country from total ruin, and Traitorous Tyrants are in place working to keep that from happening. An Atheistic, Communistic Secular Humanism has infiltrated the government, pulpits, education, courts, media, and Hollywood, and it puts our posterity at risk of slavery, death, and eternal damnation.

As Thomas Jefferson penned in the Original Declaration of Independence: That to secure these Rights, Governments are instituted among men, deriving their just powers from the consent of the governed, that whenever any form of Government becomes destructive of these ends, it is the Right of the people to alter or to abolish it, and to institute new Government, laying its foundation on such principles, and organizing its powers in such form, as to them shall seem most likely to effect their safety and happiness.

    This is a call to Shepherds, ministry leaders, and Christians from all walks of life, that understand the times. We need real men like the ones Jesus was with to form this Christian nation, and to connect with other Christian Patriots that understand the times we live in. What are you willing to do for the lives and souls of those around you? Are you willing to make any efforts yourself, like pray, fast, humble yourself, and seek HIS face, which God requires? How about looking up a few verses, but don't stop with what I give you, John 4:16, Hosea 4:6-8, Luke 11:23, James 4:17, Acts 5:29, Ezek. 33, Jeremiah 17:5-10, Proverbs 6:16-19, Ecc. 9:10. You can email Coach Dave Daubenmire or Dr. Gregory Thompson at christianminutemenunited@yahoo.com the children's lives, minds, and souls are at risk and you are called.

    Remember in the Declaration of Independence...But when a long train of abuses and usurpations, pursuing invariably the same object, evinces a design to reduce them under absolute despotism, it is their right, it is their duty, to throw off such government and to provide new guards for their future security. We have had a long train of abuses and usurpations, to take Christianity out of our country, to make Christians cower so that a new world view can put man on a throne as god, destroying the virtues of children and families. Jesus gave up everything out of love for us. What are we prepared to do out of love for Him and the children? A Declaration of Dependence upon God will make you an enemy to the world, but a friend to God. It will mean giving everything including your life, out of love for God and for HIS children.

05/15/2009

27

ARMED BUT NOT DANGEROUS VS. DANGEROUS BUT NOT ARMED

Men, what a joy you must have in your heart, to know that God has picked you from eternity for this moment in time. A friend of mine put it something like this, you have decided to make a stand against the uncircumcised Philistines. Like David you are willing to stand against those that are threatening and causing harm to God's children. I ask that you give the passion of the Holy Spirit to each of HIS children, so that they will hear, and they will watch each of us as leaders, so we can never RETREAT! Lay your foundation on Jesus, tell the people what has happened, what is happening, what to expect in the future, what we can do, give a revival, an awakening, and hope from the Gospel of Jesus Christ. If you can, mention the darkness spread by the dupes of Satan, shine light on their evil. Glorify God in all that you do and He will honor those efforts. We must warn the people and stir them to action for HIS honor and glory, allowing HIM to use each of us as a vessel to bring souls to Him. let us each cage our tongues and ask that Jesus speak through you with His wisdom.

You, He made alive, who ... once walked according to the course of this world... you ought to walk and to please Go. (Ephesians 2.1-2; 1 Thessalonians 4.1).

When we become Christians we are commanded to repent from our former worldview and lifestyle, but that does not mean that we are on our own to invent what we imagine is an acceptable Christian lifestyle. The Jews were cast aside by Jehovah, and He turned to the Gentiles, because they refused to commit themselves to the gospel. Instead, they sought to establish their own righteousness by establishing numerous laws in their Talmud, and it was the man-inspired Talmud, not the God-inspired Old Testament that the Priests memorized and taught. Are we not attempting the same thing today by approaching our cultural issues from our perspective instead of analyzing them from God's perspective?

Neither does it mean that we are to mentally assent to the truths of Scripture without having any inclination of incorporating the biblical truths we learn into our world and life view. Jesus expects us to commit our complete lifestyle to following His perfect ethical standard of behavior. The following words from the apostle John should prove more than a little alarming to those who are going through life according to their own drumbeat:

"Remember therefore from where you have fallen; repent and do the first works, Or else I will come to you quickly and remove your lamp stand from its place unless you repent" (Revelation 2.5).

The old bumper sticker: "God said it. I believe it, and that settles it," needs to have one line added to it: "and I'm going to do something about it!"

While it is impossible for us to "put" Jesus into others, we can let them see Jesus in us, by presenting a daily antithesis (and a biblical antidote) for the current non-Christian cultural agenda. God promises that if we will do that, He will bless our obedience by motivating our non-Christian neighbors to ask us why we live the way we do and receive the blessings that we do (Deuteronomy 4.5-9).

How can we love God with all our heart, soul and mind unless we give all of our effort? Matthew 23.37; 1 Corinthians 10.31

Excel in all things. 1 Corinthians 14.11-13; Proverbs 22.28-29

Whatever your hand finds to do, do it with your might; for there is no work or device or knowledge or wisdom in the grave where you are going. Ecclesiastes 9.10

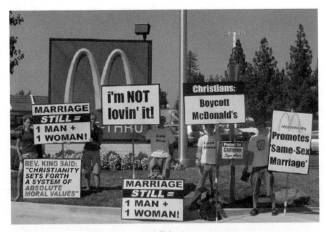

28

CORRECTION OF MODERN DAY PREACHERS

What if our modern day TV preachers were faced with the decision that all of the apostles were faced with? Over and over, they were warned to stop preaching in that Name. They were beaten within an inch of their lives many times, yet they continued to lift up the name of Jesus. For all but one of them, this faithfulness ended in a martyr's death. The only exception was the Apostle John who was boiled in oil and survived. He was then banished to the island of Patmos where he died of old age in a prison camp.

Not only did the apostles face incredible persecution. There are historical documents testifying of women who, rather than denying their Lord, were forced to watch their own children thrown to lions. To many of us, these are just stories, right? The truth is, you will never know what you would do unless put in that situation. All we can do is die to ourselves every day, in order that maybe, just maybe, God would give us the grace to stand in that day.

Dying to ourselves? Ha! Where are you going to hear that preached today? We live in an age where the prophets are not teaching us to deny ourselves and follow Christ. They are not teaching us to take upon ourselves the responsibility of the birthright. No! They only appeal to our own monstrous lusts. "Get your blessing," they cry. In essence they are proclaiming, "It's all about ME!" And now, a generation has risen up, who deny their birthright, and follow after the blessing. How foolish we are!

Where are the true prophets? Where are the watchmen? Where are the men of God that will tear down the arguments of these foolish preachers? The message is not, nor has it ever been, "How to live your life to the fullest!" No! Quite the contrary, the message of the gospel has always been, "How to die well!" You will find that all through the Scriptures.

I could give you a long list of these false prophets who claim that the gospel is all about life enhancement. Likewise, I could give you a long list of true prophets who preach the true gospel, that the only way to find your life is to lose it. However, for the most part, both are to blame for the awful state of the church, and both are to blame for the awful state of this nation, and the awful state of the families and children. While the false prophets are leading the sheep astray, many of the true prophets are leading the sheep...nowhere!

God has given us His Word. He has given us many resources to study His Word. He has given us great minds to learn and teach His Word. But He has also given us our bodies to do His Word. *James 1:22 says, "Do not merely listen to the word, and so deceive yourselves. Do what it says."* Adam Tennant is a loving servant warrior for Christ and HIS absolute Truth.

Jesus said, *"All power is given unto Me in heaven and earth. Go you therefore, and teach all nations, baptizing them in the name of the Father, and of the Son, and of the Holy Ghost: Teaching them to observe all things whatsoever I have commanded you: and, lo, I am with you always, even unto the end of the world"* (Matthew 28:18-20).

What are you waiting for? To know this and to say you have been reborn, how does it hold that Christians and Shepherds do nothing? You might say, what do you mean, do nothing? We send some money to missions, we have wonderful committee meetings, we give food to the local pantry, and we are involved in all the mercy ministries, but to know what to do and to not do it, is it not said to be a sin by God? As children's souls are at risk of going to hell for eternity and children are murdered daily, do you think it will be a good idea to hang on to the thought that you will tell Jesus you fed the hungry, clothed the naked, while children went to hell? Will Jesus tell many sleeping Christians to go over with the goats, that He does not know you? Then what will He do to the hired Shepherds?

I judge none of your hearts. Jesus has given me a gift to love you, but you must judge yourself, before Jesus does. I do judge out of love, your actions or lack of. Look around you; do you not understand the times at all? Are you willing to hear a prophetic warning, or do you just want your best life now? Do you want the truth, or just to feel good?

Every Shepherd, pastor and priest, that does not tell his flock to get their children out of the government schools is sinning and putting themselves at risk of going to hell for eternity. Every elder that does not warn the pastor and the people about getting out of the government schools is sinning and putting themselves at risk of going to hell for eternity. Every Christian sitting in the pews that does not warn the pastor and elders and the people setting in the pews to get their children out of the government schools is putting them at risk of going to hell for eternity. There are so many, start by reading Matthew 18:6,7.

The government school, yes government, because they are no longer public, as they indoctrinate the children in an ungodly and pagan environment full of lies, and socializing them to be good little comrades. Even though it was never meant biblically to put our children into a public school, at one time they at least tried to keep God a strong part of the education of the child so that they could recognize the counterfeit leaders we have in our government today, and would quickly put them out of service to the people.

Jesus told you to "Seek first HIS kingdom" and those going to His kingdom will love God with all their hearts, minds, souls, and strength, and love their neighbor as themselves. Do not say that you love Jesus if you are putting the children at risk for eternity in an indoctrination system that is against God, family, and country.

Please, (Shepherds) priests, pastors, elders, and Christians laity, do not deceive yourselves. Your children are at great risk when attending a government k-12 and a government college, and be very careful of those that claim to be Christian, because of your silence, the world in Satan's control has crept into the Christian colleges and universities.. I know that many have made this Sacred Cow an Idol, and those that understand the urgency for the children must pray for those with strongholds that keep them from seeing and hearing. Love and prayers in Christ to each of you.

—Gregory

Shepherds, did you vote Republican, Democrat, or Christocrat. The first two work for Satan, so what will you do now. This is the mission of a friend of mine, Buddy Hanson, "To make Satan's worst nightmare come true by assisting Christian legislators in 'connect their Spiritual Dots' to their daily decision-making and 'walk their talk' by framing the cultural debate according to God's ideas vs. Man's ideas, instead of according to conservative man's ideas vs. liberal man's ideas, because once God is taken out of the cultural debate only non-Christians ideas will prevail." Since God's Word is Truth, and any decision (legislative or otherwise) that does not conform to biblical principles is false and will not be successful, regardless of how much time, effort and/or money is thrown at it.

Understand Shepherds, that if you vote for the least of two evils, you are sinning against God, thinking that by being pragmatic you can get around

God's commands. If you don't give this warning to your people, you are also sinning and will have their blood on your hands. Did you possibly see in your Bible which you indicate is the inerrant Word of God, that Jesus said, "I am the Way, and the Truth, and the Life. No one comes to the Father except through Me" (John 14:6). Jesus alone is the "Voice of Truth.

Elaine Graham carries her cross, along with truth, to the State House on Tuesday

29

The Church Isn't Ready for Revival!

By David Wilkerson February 20, 1995: There are two kinds of churches in the world today. First, there is the dead, formal church, which has a form of godliness but no power. Its ministers are hirelings, most of whom are unconverted. God calls such shepherds "...twice dead..." (Jude12). And He promises to pluck up such churches by the roots and burn them!

I have preached in several of these lifeless mausoleums over the years. The pastors would invite me because they had read "The Cross and the Switchblade." Yet whenever I preached in such a church, and the Holy Spirit fell upon me, the pastor grew nervous, slumping in his seat. People would be weeping under Holy-Ghost conviction. But as soon as I gave an invitation, the pastor stepped in quickly and dismissed the meeting.

Oh, how that bothered me! Those pastors dreaded the very thought of anyone having an emotional response to my preaching. All they wanted was to get the people up off their knees and out the door before the Holy Ghost could do something "out of control." We know God cannot bless such churches with revival, because He doesn't pour out His Spirit where He is not welcome. And the dead, formal church has rejected the Holy Ghost outright. It simply does not want to be raised from the dead. But there is another kind of church in the world today. And that is a holy, remnant church—a praying, God-fearing, uncompromising, righteous body of believers. It is comprised of people wholly given to Christ—people who pray, fast and seek the face of God regularly.

My message is concerned primarily with this righteous, Holy-Ghost church. Why? It is the only church in a position to receive a great outpouring of the Holy Spirit! You see, God pours out His Spirit only on those who ask Him to come, and who prepare themselves to receive Him. Yet I do not believe the true church is ready for revival—for God's last, great, promised outpouring of His Spirit. You see, a church can be engrossed for months in prayer, fasting, weeping, supplications, begging and beseeching the Holy Ghost to fall—and yet still may not be ready for revival!

(Let me explain the terms I'm using here: The word revival literally means "the resurrection of that which threatens to become a corpse." So, if you revive someone, it means he has already passed out. Yet I do not believe God's holy, remnant church has fainted. And when I use the word revival, I'm actually talking about an outpouring of God's Spirit.)

It is necessary to search God's Word to find out how His people prepared themselves. You see, God has given us many biblical promises that are "on call"—that is, ready to be fulfilled. And I believe He is simply waiting on a people who will prepare themselves to lay hold of these promises. Of course, God is sovereign and can pour out His Spirit on anyone He chooses. There are reports of the Holy Ghost falling on various peoples around the world, bringing resurrection life to those who neither expected it nor were prepared for it. Yet God also gives us a biblical pattern that shows us His standard and way. And His way is this: He works through a prepared people! He digs up fallow ground before He sets things in divine order.

I want to give you three reasons why I believe the church is not ready for revival. I pray that as we look at these, we will line up with God's Word in preparation to receive what He has promised:

1. **We are not ready for revival if we are convinced this society has sinned away its day of grace!** America has so grieved God—its intensity of sin is so horrible—that many are convinced there is no hope left! Indeed, in recent years I have been nearly convinced by America's terrible moral landslide that God has no option left but judgment. So I have preached His impending judgments intensely, especially over the past ten years. And I still believe that message with all my heart—and will continue preaching it with all authority! You see, God may wait patiently for repentance, sending many prophets to warn of judgment. But a day finally comes when He says, "Enough!" I call this "the dread release," when God releases a society to destructive judgments. We see several examples of this in church history.

    It happened to Noah's generation. God strove with wicked mankind for 120 years, with mercy, warnings and visible signs such as the ark. But finally He said, "No more!" And He wiped out all of humanity, except for those who entered the ark. It happened also to Lot's generation, in Sodom and Gomorrah. God counted the days of wickedness in that society so saturated with homosexuality, lust and violence. Finally He could endure no more and said, "Your cup of iniquity is full. Your sins have ascended to heaven!" And He wiped out those cities and all the surrounding towns. They were given over to "the dread release!" It happened as well in Jerusalem. Christ walked the streets of that city and wept, warning of the coming judgment. Seventy years later, God said, "That's enough!" And Jerusalem fell, razed to the ground. Thousands were murdered in a horrible holocaust. God put this same message in the heart of Jeremiah. He sent the prophet to the gates of the temple with this solemn cry: *"But go ye now unto my place which was in Shiloh, where I set my name at the first, and see what I did to it for the wickedness of my people Israel.... Therefore will I do unto this house, which is called by my name, wherein ye trust, and unto the place which I gave to you and to your fathers, as I have done to Shiloh.... Therefore pray not thou for this people, neither lift up cry nor prayer for them, neither make intercession to me: for I will not hear thee"* (Jeremiah 7:12-16).

God told the righteous, "You can stop praying now! My patience is gone, and I have determined judgment. I'm going to take My Spirit from the east gate and lift it from My house completely. It's going to be just like Shiloh!" Shiloh stands as a testimony to all generations that judgment begins in God's house. God's people had become so backslidden and wicked that the Lord moved in with sudden and awesome judgments. Shiloh was where the Spirit of God departed, and "Ichabod" was written above the door. The Lord removed all His glory, shut the doors and departed—leaving it in ruin!

The Word of the Lord also came to Ezekiel with the same kind of warning: *"Son of man, when the land sinneth against me by trespassing grievously, then will I stretch out mine hand upon it, and will break the staff of the bread thereof, and will send famine upon it, and will cut off man and beast from it: Though these three men, Noah, Daniel, and Job, were in it, they should deliver but their own souls by their righteousness, saith the Lord God... They shall deliver neither son nor daughter; they shall but deliver their own souls by their righteousness"* (Ezekiel 14:13-14, 20).

God was saying, "Even these three men—Noah, Daniel and Job— couldn't pray down a revival. Even their righteous prayers couldn't buy more time. You see, I determine judgment—and all the praying people in the world can't change My mind!" When I see what God did to Noah's generation, Sodom and Jerusalem, I can't help but deduct that America is ripe for destruction!

Think about it for a moment: None of those societies killed over 50 million babies, as we have through abortion. Their inhabitants didn't commit random acts of murder in their streets in such aggregate numbers as we do today. Sodom's entire population didn't equal the number of gays who recently marched in one parade in New York City. Beloved, we are a million times worse than those generations, and God judged and destroyed them all! I often pray, "Oh, God, if You destroyed them, how can You spare us? Why have Your fierce judgments been held back from America?" Experts say the economy is booming in this year of 1995. Our gross national product is increasing. Automobile factories are producing cars at a record-breaking pace. Inflation is holding steadily. Indeed, everything looks good ahead. Yet, why doesn't all this good news bring any sense of security to people? All across the country, people feel that something is hanging in the air, about to happen. Even the worst sinner doesn't feel secure. Why? It is because, deep down, this nation knows it deserves judgment! We all know we're living on borrowed time. How can we be ready for revival if we believe that all hope is gone—that we have sinned away our day of grace and there is nothing left but judgment? Beloved, we can't have faith for a revival until we're convinced God still wants to pour out His Spirit on us! Why hasn't America been judged? Why hasn't Jesus come yet? It is because there is still a great harvest ahead! And God is *"...not willing that any should perish, but that all should come to repentance"* (2 Peter 3:9).

We see this great mercy of the Lord in a passage in Isaiah. God instructed the prophet to tell Judah: *"Thus saith the Lord, Where is the bill of your mother's divorcement, whom I have put away? Or which of my creditors is it to whom I have sold you? Behold, for your iniquities have ye sold yourselves, and for your transgressions is your mother put away. Wherefore, when I came, was there no man? When I called, was there none to answer? Is my hand shortened at all, that it cannot redeem? or have I no power to deliver?"* (Isaiah 50:1-2). God had already divorced Israel, giving them *"...a bill of divorce..."* (Jeremiah 3:8). But now His attention was on Judah, a people who had cheated on Him and walked away from Him. God still had a heart for Judah, and He came to them crying, *"Where is the bill of..divorcement..."* (Isaiah 50:1). He was saying, "Show Me your divorce papers! Prove to me I ever put you away. It was you who walked away from Me! I did nothing to grieve or hurt you. I loved you the whole time. I came to you and I called you!"

Try to picture it: There was the Lord, going into the very dens of Judah's harlotry to look for her, calling, "I'm coming after you! You're telling everyone that there's no hope, that there can never again be a love between us. But I'm coming back for you!" Beloved, that is exactly what I see God doing with America right now. He is saying to us, "Show Me your divorce papers! Show Me I walked away from you! I have not yet removed My Holy Spirit. Rather, I am still at work all over this nation—still wooing, calling, coming to you!" The Lord is speaking this through Times Square Church and many other pulpits across this nation. And He is speaking it through godly men and women who spend precious time seeking Him. He is calling America back to repentance -back to His own heart! Yet, when He comes, He asks, "Where are those who will answer My call? Where are those who will return to Me?"

This is what our recent weeks of prayer at Times Square Church have been about. It all has to do with His last call! Many who sit in our church are proof of the Lord's wooing. At one time He stirred their hearts and shook them out of apostasy and compromise. He called out, "I love you!" And they responded. And now the same Spirit who roused them wants to gather in a whole multitude. Our part is to pray with faith that, as the Spirit woos backsliders, a multitude will answer and return. We have to be fully persuaded that there is still time (though short), still hope—and that while we are praying, the Spirit is at work in all levels of society, calling and wooing people to Himself!

2. **We Are Not Ready for Revival When We Are Overwhelmed by the Darkness That Has Settled Over the Nation and by the Fury of the Enemy!** I see a fury and an intensity in sinners today as in no other generation. When I was a boy, the church referred to Africa as "the dark continent" because of its spiritual darkness. But today, a spiritual darkness is hovering over America that is almost tangible. America is now "the dark continent"! "For, behold, the darkness shall cover the earth, and gross darkness the people..." (Isaiah 60:2). "Gross darkness" signifies a darkness you can feel. And the darkness over America right now is intense, widespread, thickening every moment. When you fly into New York, you're dazzled by all the city's bright lights. Yet, once you get off the plane, take a cab into Manhattan and get out at Broadway, you instantly feel the darkness. It's heavy, demonic, blinding people's hearts and minds—and it's getting worse!

Yet, the Bible says God has a part in that darkness: *"Give glory to the Lord your God, before he cause darkness, and before your feet stumble upon the dark mountains, and, while ye look for light, he turn it into the shadow of death, and make it gross darkness"* (Jeremiah 13:16). God makes the gross darkness! When people are so set on their sin that they reject the Lord, they are driven to darkness. David said of the wicked, *"Let their eyes be darkened, that they see not..."* (Psalm 69:23). The Spirit of God allows a darkness to fall over their hearts and minds.

"And they shall look unto the earth; and behold trouble and darkness, dimness of anguish; and they shall be driven to darkness" (Isaiah 8:22). Sinners are actually driven to their dark acts. Satan has come down upon the earth with an army of demonic powers who are whipping godless people into a frenzy of evil! The fury and intensity of this present vileness is a thousand times darker than when I first came to New York a generation ago.

Today I look at people's eyes as they're on their way to make a drug connection, stumbling out of a bar, running to and fro looking for pleasure—and there is no mistaking they are driven! When I first began this ministry some thirty-five years ago, I spoke in churches all over America, warning of the moral landslide to come. I told people in Iowa, Oklahoma and all the Southern states that drugs would strike even the smallest hamlet. Pushers would appear in schools and on playgrounds. I warned of blatant homosexuality, with nude parades taking place in our cities. And I prophesied that nudity and sexual acts would air on prime-time TV. Most of the people who heard me thought I'd come from Mars. Pastors berated me. And sincere Christians came to me afterward, saying, "No way! God will never let that happen to America." Today, some of those people who ridiculed me are grandparents. They sit before their TV watching the R-rated, perverted movies I prophesied about. And their children and grandchildren are addicted to drugs and alcohol.

The darkness I warned about has now come into their very souls! Can you imagine how dark it's going to be ten years from now, should the Lord tarry? Yet, I ask you: As you see the darkness thickening and growing on all sides, do you believe it will exceed the light of the gospel? Are you afraid the darkness is going to squash it, quell it, snuff it out? No—never! God's people must never be intimidated by the darkness and fury of the enemy in these last days. It doesn't matter how dark the world becomes. The Bible says Jesus is going to rise and shine in the darkness!

"I, even I, am he that comforteth you: who art thou, that thou shouldest be

afraid of a man that shall die, and of the son of man which shall be made as grass; and forgettest the Lord thy maker, that hath stretched forth the heavens, and laid the foundations of the earth; and hast feared continually every day because of the fury of the oppressor, as if he were ready to destroy? and where is the fury of the oppressor?" (Isaiah 51:12-13).—*"Yea, the darkness hideth not from thee; but the night shineth as the day: the darkness and the light are both alike to thee"* (Psalm 139:12).—*"...he knoweth what is in the darkness, and the light dwelleth with him"* (Daniel 2:22).—*"The people that walked in darkness have seen a great light: they that dwell in the land of the shadow of death, upon them hath the light shined"* (Isaiah 9:2). We live in a time of widespread death and darkness. But God says that in such times He will shine His light the brightest: *"And I will bring the blind by a way that they knew not; I will lead them in paths that they have not known: I will make darkness light before them, and crooked things straight. These things will I do unto them, and not forsake them"* (Isaiah 42:16).

It doesn't matter how wild it gets in the streets, or how many homosexuals curse Christ in gay parades. We are not to be overwhelmed by any darkness! When gross darkness covers the earth, we must expect the Lord to shine in all His glory and to deliver multitudes: *"Arise, shine; for thy light is come, and the glory of the Lord is risen upon thee. For, behold, the darkness shall cover the earth, and gross darkness the people: but the Lord shall arise upon thee, and his glory shall be seen upon thee. And the Gentiles shall come to thy light, and kings to the brightness of thy rising"* (Isaiah 60:1-3). No darkness will ever stop God's light! So get your eyes off the darkness, off the sin, off the fury of violent people. And believe the Lord for the bursting forth of His shining, effusing light!

3. The Church Is Not Ready for Revival Because of Its Weak Faith In God's Willingness and Power to Save Wicked, Hardened Sinners!
God put His finger on Judah's problem: They doubted His willingness and power to redeem a people entrenched in apostasy and idolatry. *"And they said, There is no hope: but we will walk after our own devices, and we will every one do the imagination of his evil heart"* (Jeremiah 18:12). Judah had given up hope, thinking, "We've gone too far—and now there's no going back. We have left the Lord, mocked Him, abused Him, cast Him aside. We are so deep into our sins, it's hopeless. Not even God can bring us back!"

Beloved, after all my years in ministry, I still have to fight this kind of thinking. You may feel the same way. Your husband may be an atheist, mean and godless. And you have convinced yourself, "All around me, people are getting saved. But my husband is different.

He's so hard!" The Lord said to Judah, *"...Is my hand shortened at all, that it cannot redeem?..."* (Isaiah 50:2). To shorten means to "chop off." God was saying, "Tell me—has the enemy chopped off My mighty arm? Have I lost My power to save? No! My mighty arm dried up the Red Sea. It clothed the heavens with blackness. It opened blind eyes. You have seen that I save to the uttermost. Why do you think I have lost My power to redeem you?"

Dear saint, when did God lose His power to save the vilest sinner on earth? When did He lose His willingness to deliver drug addicts, drunkards and prostitutes, when nobody was praying for them? Would God then somehow decide not to save your family members, for whom you have fasted and prayed faithfully? Absolutely not! We must cry out to Him in faith, "Oh Lord, You can save Wall Street. You can deliver the worst homosexual in New York. You can redeem any Muslim in any foreign land. And you can save any member of my family. Your arm is not too short. You can save anybody!" We will never be ready for revival until we stop limiting God. Don't believe His hand has been chopped off; instead, believe Him for the impossible! Get a vision of His mercy and love—of His mighty, outstretched arm, all-powerful to save!

If Jesus prophesied a great harvest, then we are going to witness supernatural outpourings of God's Spirit on vast multitudes. When the Spirit was poured out the first time in Jerusalem, thousands were saved at once. And, likewise today, we ought to pray with faith for the Spirit to fall on entire nations even those with incredible strongholds.

In recent years, the Holy Spirit has moved in China, and great multitudes there have been saved. Isaiah prophesies of many people being gathered in from Sinim, which represents China: *"Behold, these shall come from far: and, lo, these from the north and from the west; and these from the land of Sinim"* (Isaiah 49:12). That same Holy-Ghost fire is also falling in Russia and in parts of India. God's Spirit is moving, wooing, calling people all over the world! Yet God is asking His remnant church to begin with our own families, one person at a time: *"Turn, O backsliding children, saith the Lord; for I am married unto you: and I will take you one of a city, and two of a family, and I will bring you to Zion"* (Jeremiah 3:14). We are to pray and be patient—and He will gather in our loved ones, one at a time!

Here at Times Square Church, we are praying that God will sweep many into His kingdom through outpourings of His Spirit. But the Lord also wants us to focus on our families. We must have an urgency in us to pray, "Lord, send conviction on my family! Save my son, my daughter, my wife..." Several years ago there was a popular song, "Raindrops Keep Fallin' on My Head." I believe that song tells us the way we ought to pray—for God to literally rain down His Holy Spirit!

Scripture promises that in the last days, the Holy Ghost will fall as rain. And you can pray Holy-Ghost raindrops down upon the heads of your loved ones: *"Ask ye of the Lord rain in the time of the latter rain; so the Lord shall make bright clouds, and give them showers of rain, to every one grass in the field"* (Zechariah 10:1). God is waiting and anxious to pour out His Holy Ghost. Are you ready to pray down His rain? We are to pray not for the fire of judgment, but for rain! Yes, God's judgment is coming; it is at the door even now. But while we still have time, we are to believe God to pour out His Spirit. So lay hold of His divine, "on call" promises—and you will see a Holy-Ghost revival poured out all around you. Hallelujah!

Multitudes of Christians including pastors, deacons, ministry people of all kinds are losing their faith and confidence in the power of Jesus' name! They are turning away from Christ as the answer to everything. They are falling away from a childlike faith in Him alone as the solution to all life's problems. There is a wholesale turning toward methods, toward psychology, toward human expertise, toward the philosophies and doctrines of men. This was directed to the leaders of Israel, under Hezekiah—but also to the church of these latter days.

Drug abuse, alcoholism, adultery, gambling, homosexuality, fornication, pornography—all these evil deeds are sins against the flesh, against society, and against the laws and commandments of God. But this sin is against the Lord Himself it is a personal indignity against a Holy God! Keep in mind—this is our grieved Lord who is speaking: *"You now make your plans without consulting Me!" "You are now in league with those who lean on the arm of flesh, and not the Spirit!" "You are going back to the very thing I delivered you from—back to seeking help from what once caused you all your pain and bondage." "Woe to those who go down to Egypt for help, who rely on horses, and trust in chariots because they are many, and in horsemen because they are very strong, but they do not look to the Holy One of Israel, nor seek the Lord!"* (Isaiah 31:1)

Remember this is all about how to be delivered from the enemy! It has to do with deliverance! How do we deliver God's people from the raging enemies! The Assyrians are at the gate, threatening destruction. Assyria means successful enemy. This represents the on-rushing tide of evil that seems to be so successful today! How are God's leaders—His shepherds—His elders going to face this formidable enemy at the gate? He has swept away everything before him; it seems as if he is unstoppable. Israel Panicked! They got their eyes on the enemy they did not turn to the Lord with full confidence and trust! They turned to the arm of the flesh. They sent ambassadors to Egypt, to the government leaders and generals in Zoan and Hanes.

They took matters in their own hands. Isaiah paints a vivid picture of the emptiness and anguish ahead of them. In going down to Egypt they were headed *"Through a land of distress and anguish, where dwells the lion, viper and serpent." They would find nothing but emptiness, vanity. "Therefore, I have called her Rahab who has been exterminated"* (Isaiah 30:7). Rahab here in Hebrew is, 'I have called Egypt, Greatmouth that sits still?' Others render it, "The Bragging people who are idlers." (Keil, Delitzsch). The picture is terrible: Here are God's people, going backwards through the same desert they had been delivered from, returning for help to a boastful, bragging world system that could not move! They were willing to once again endure emptiness, pain, anguish—in a wilderness, looking to the world for help.

Look at the church today; look at its armies of trained experts; look at its shepherds and workers. Where are most of them headed? Back to the wilderness, back to Great-Mouth Egypt! Turning away from the Man of Galilee; away from the reproach of the Cross; away from the power of prayer; away from faith; away from the Word of God. *"For this is a rebellious people who refuse to listen to the instructions of the lord"* (Isaiah 30:9).

Moses prophesied this very thing would happen in the latter days! He foretold of the great falling away of God's people. *"Take this book of the law and place it beside the Ark of the Covenant of the Lord your God, that it may remain there as a witness against you. For I know your rebellion and your stubbornness; behold, while I am still alive with you today, you have been rebellious against the Lord; how much more, then, after my death? Assemble to me all the elders of your tribes and your officers, that I may speak these words in their hearing and call the heavens and the earth to witness against them. For I know that after my death you will act corruptly and turn from the way which I have commanded you; and evil will befall you in the latter days, for you will do that which is evil in the sight of the Lord, provoking Him to anger with the work of your hands"* (Deuteronomy 31:26-29). He warned, "You will turn away—evil will befall you in the latter days". Moses prophesied: *"When I bring them into the land flowing with milk and honey, which I swore to their fathers, and they have eaten and become prosperous, then they will turn to other gods and serve them, and spurn me and break my covenant".* (Deuteronomy 31:20).

Let's tie it down and get to the point the prophets are making. What does it mean to spurn the Lord to go down to Egypt? How does that interpret in these latter days? God is saying, "When you were first called—when I touched you and delivered you from the enemy, you wanted only Me! You prayed about everything! You had a childlike trust and faith in Me, that I would guide you, that I would miraculously supply all your needs. I was your joy—I alone was your satisfaction. You were not burned out; you had a yearning heart after Me! "Now you have all your experts, your how-to books. You have modern methods. You don't need Me to supply your need now. You have experts to tell you how to raise money, how to write letters, how to make appeals. You have seminars, training sessions, more experts, and more advice, much of which incorporates the teachings of this world. You are learning how to do things better, but getting to know Me less! I am not the center of it all now, you do it in My name, busily engaged, hard working—but it leaves you weary, burned out, empty, because you are on the road to Egypt. You are headed in the wrong direction.

Our churches no longer have the power of God to attract the people. They go down to Egypt, borrow its music, its dancing, it's entertainment, hoping for a crowd! No passion for souls—just crowds! Church growth at any cost! Look at the average church bulletin; it looks like a theater calendar. The church wants to ride the swift horses of Egypt! It is a stench in God's nostrils. Even the para-church ministries are falling away, apostatizing! Workers are parked in front of the TV idol. Many are reading psychology books. While some still have a passion for souls, even that often becomes worldly hype and human energy"!

1. **There Will Follow a Rejection of the Message of Holiness, Judgment and Repentance!** *"Who say to the seers, You must not see visions! And to the*

prophets, You must not prophesy to us what is right. Speak to us pleasant words, prophesying illusions" (Isaiah 30:10). An apostate church wants nothing to do with the visions or prophecies of men of righteousness. They want no message that disturbs, no upsetting of their successful world. They refuse any kind of correction. Everything is excused under the banner of love. They clamor for entertainment! They flock by the thousands to concerts, plays, social gatherings, they ridicule prophets.

They mock what they call the Doomsday Preachers! They live with Illusions. They don't want a Preacher or Evangelist to tell them the hard truth—to bring forth the Sword of the Lord. They say, "Preach to us smooth things! Bless us! Make us happy! Make us feel good!" They especially reject the message of holiness and separation. They say, *"Get out of the way, turn aside from the paths...Let us hear no more about the Holy One of Israel"* (Isaiah 30:11). I never thought I'd live to see the day that Assembly of God Pastors would write me reproachful letters, telling me I am bringing confusion and gloom to the body of Christ. For what? Preaching holiness, judgment and repentance? Jeremiah was sent to prophesy against the apostate Jews, the Lord's own people. God warned him, *"They will fight you... the dread of the Lord is no longer in them... They prefer to drink from cisterns now, rather than living water"* (Jeremiah 1,2,3).

Why do people embrace the prosperity message and reject correction and calls to repentance and holiness? It is because of their lifestyles. Prosperity preaching fits beautifully into their successful lifestyles. They flock to those teachers, because they want to feel comfortable in their world of materialism. They are in no mood to give up anything, or to sacrifice, or to hear of crosses and losses. They are into buying, acquiring, enjoying, climbing. They refuse to heed the prophetic warnings that the party will soon be over.

An Apostate Church Simply Endures the Prophetic Voice. They pass it by with a condescending smile. And that is worse than out-right rejection. *"And they come to you as people come, and sit before you as My people, and hear your words, but they do not do them, for they do the lustful desires expressed by their mouth, and their heart goes after their gain. And behold, you are to them like a sensual song by one who has a beautiful voice and plays well on an instrument: for they hear your words, but they do not practice them"* (Ezekiel 33:31,32).

To many Christians, even those sincere, who call themselves "His people," the call to rid their home of the TV idol, to shut down Rock and Roll and Music of the Devils, to get serious about total surrender, is all a novel message. It is a little on the entertaining side to them—they love to hear it to "Amen" it, but it does not affect them. They continue to follow the lusts of their hearts. You see, they are liberated, not under law or legalism and refuse to permit the Holy Spirit to probe their inner man about its seeping corruption in their lives and homes. According to the Prophecy of Isaiah, the Apostate Church of the Last Days Will Totally Reject the Call to Repentance! *"For thus saith the Lord God, the Holy One of Israel, in repentance and rest you shall be saved, in quietness and truth is your strength. But you were not willing ... You said, no!"* (Isaiah 30:15,16).

God's message to the church now is this: "Your one last hope, your only strength left, is to return to me with all your heart; repent—Trust Me Only! Turn aside from Egypt, the world! Tell that to the multi-million dollar TV ministries! Tell that to the busy, prosperous pastors! Tell that to the money-mad crowds! Tell them that their only salvation now is in repentance and holiness!

They don't even have the time to consider the question, let alone answer it. Isaiah says they will reject the message of repentance; reject the thought of quietness, rest and simple trust—they are too busy racing about on swift horses, fleeing—chasing their own dreams.

Isaiah predicted a sudden collapse of those individuals and ministries who rejected the message of repentance. *"Therefore thus says the Holy One of Israel, Since you have rejected this Word, and have put trust in oppression and guile, and have relied on them, therefore this iniquity will be to you like a breach about to fall, a bulge in a high wall, whose collapse comes suddenly in an instant. And whose collapse is like the smashing of a potter's jar; so ruthlessly shattered"* (Is 30:12-14).

There is coming a sudden, overnight, ruthless shattering—a collapse of ministries, churches, lifestyles—of those who are at ease in Zion! I have seen what Isaiah saw! There is coming, very soon, an economic calamity, so sudden, so unexpected—the money flow will stop! TV ministries will go bankrupt one after another. Many churches which are laden with debt will fall into bankruptcy. Those who preach prosperity exclusively will become the most hated preachers in the land. Already we receive mail from those who were in that camp, but now in deep financial trouble—and the hurting ones are turning on their teacher, crying, "You deceived me! Why doesn't your stuff work now?" The teachers themselves will be in terror, beholding the collapse—overnight! Believe me, it is all about to be shattered! Is Isaiah lying? Hear him: "Because you rejected this word of holiness, repentance and prophetic warnings, your high wall will develop a bulge; it will fall suddenly—it will all be over and done in a moment!"

Who can believe it? Today, billions of dollars flow freely! They build; they buy; they sell; they go about their dreams as if it will never end! But the day is just ahead—shortly, an awesome collapse is coming! So ruthless! So shattering! So suddenly! Who would have believed the frightful collapse of the Oil Market? Who would have believed that our Shuttle would explode? Thousands of apostate shepherds and their helpless flocks will tremble in shame and terror! *"One thousand will flee at the threat of one man, you shall flee at the threat of five; until you are left as a flag on a mountain top, and as a signal on a hill"* (Isaiah 30:17). This means that fear will overcome them. They will be chased about to and fro, no hiding place, no rest, no quiet confidence, no inner strength—terrorized! They will become just a shadow of what once was!

The kingdom of self, of pride, of ambition, is coming down! The warnings of Isaiah will not be heeded—my warnings will be scoffed at. But they have been warned! When it comes, and it will, what good will their message then be? Who will listen? Their dreams and illusions will be swept away! Their stages of entertainment decimated! Even the ungodly will say, "How could it be? Why has God done this to them?" These warnings will not trouble those Christians who are shut in with God. The warnings of Jesus were stronger than the warnings just read—yet to the trusting ones He said, *"Fear not."* Read on saints there is a glorious side to it all!

2. **Out of the Apostate Church Will Arise a Holy, Repentant People Who Will Yearn After the Lord!** How our Lord yearns to have a people here who long for Him only! He grieves over the apostate thing, but His compassion will bring forth a people who return, who repent—who want only Him! *"Therefore the Lord longs to be gracious to you. And therefore He waits on high to have compassion on you. For the Lord is a God of justice; How blessed are all those who long for Him"* (Isaiah 30:18). Isaiah was addressing now a people of the future! He was speaking to a people who would make up the spiritual Zion—Jerusalem, which can never fall or collapse. It is a holy people whose main characteristic is their yearning hearts after God!

What was the mark of the apostate people? They did not yearn for the Lord, but longed after Egypt, the world, the flesh, the earthly. This is

144

the sad lack of the church today! There is so little of this deep longing for Christ. There is so little of this deep longing of being shut in with Him, desiring Him as the fullness of life. We have a generation who will work for Him, we will witness, feed the poor, help the homeless, and minister to human need, but so few spend their days yearning for Him. God said, *"My people have forgotten Me days without number"* (Jeremiah 2:32). While all around there will be collapse and weeping—this people will not weep!

God is going to hear their cry and answer their prayer! *"O people in Zion, inhabitant in Jerusalem, you will weep no longer. He will surely be gracious to you at the sound of your cry; when He hears it, He will answer you"* (Ezekiel 30:19). There will be privations! There will be oppression from Satan, from the world, from circumstances, but God will be manifest among this people. The presence of the Lord will be precious to them. *"Although the Lord has given you bread of privation and water of oppression, He, your Teacher will no longer hide Himself, but your eyes will behold your teacher"* (Isaiah30:20).

3. **There Will Come Forth a Pure, Clear and Holy Word.** God will supply this people with true revelation. They will see what no others have seen! They will be led step by step by the Lord! There will be no famine of the true Word then, no more need for sermon CD's or far off seminars. The Lord already has in place an array of holiness and repentant preachers, awaiting the hour Christians will be ready to listen. No longer will they be maligned and ostracized—they will stand in the gap and proclaim the holy and pure word of the Lord to a trembling nation. *"And your ears will hear a word behind you, this is the way, walk in it, whenever you turn to the right or to the left"* (Isaiah 30:21). This people will tear down all their idols! They will so yearn after their Lord, all the idols must go! *"And you will defile your graven images, overlaid with silver, and your molten images plated with gold. You will scatter them as an impure thing; and say to them, be gone"* (Isaiah 30:22). They will enjoy their greatest ministry when all around is fear, failure and shattering collapses. *"Then He will give you rain for the seed which you will sow in the ground, and bread from the yield of the ground, and it will be rich and plenteous; on that day your livestock will graze in a roomy pasture"* (Isaiah 30:23). Praise God!

This yearning remnant will have a glorious harvest in the day of ruin and calamity! They will not be running and hiding! They heard the sound of the trumpet and prepared. They hid themselves in Christ, the cleft of the rock. For the past few years, and now in greater intensity, God has and is preparing a people He will call upon in the day of slaughter! They will not be shaken when all else is shaken by God. They will have that quiet rest and strength. They will have confidence in Him! They will not burn out! They will not be discouraged or cast down! There will be no confusion in them! They will know God has prepared them for this hour. They will be drinking from divine springs of water! *"And on every lofty mountain and on every high hill there will be streams running with water on the day of the great slaughter, when the towers fall"* (Isaiah 30:25).

Do you believe that? In the day God tears down all the strongholds which men and the apostate church trusted in, when the great slaughter of man-centered ministries begins, they will be quietly drinking from streams of supernatural water! Best of all, these bruised but trusting, yearning saints will come into the greatest, brightest revelation of Jesus Christ ever given to mankind. *"And the light of the moon will be as the light of the sun, and the light of the sun will be seven times brighter, like the light of seven days, on the day the Lord binds up the fracture of his people and heals the bruise He has inflicted"* (Isaiah 30:26).

Each remaining day before Christ returns—this repentant, trusting, yearning people will behold Him with ever-increasing light! This body will enjoy a revelation of Jesus Christ seven times more intense than all past revelations. We will meet Him, as His bride, clothed in His brightness. If this message frightens or troubles you—better search your heart! This is not a message of doom or gloom to overcomers. Those who are trusting the Lord fully will rejoice—for our day of redemption draws near! I am one of the most excited preachers in the world! I can hardly contain my joy—because God is about to bring down, and shake apart, all that is of the world and the flesh! Saints—rejoice with me!

Well a message of warning and a message of hope, and you get to choose. Do it your own way or man's way and die, or do it the Lord's way and live. I am going to kneel down and pray for you right now before I ask the Holy Spirit for more things that will help in your journey toward eternity. In HIS Service

-Gregory

"I have spoken openly to the world," Jesus replied. "I always taught in synagogues or at the temple, where all the Jews come together. I said nothing in secret. Why question me? Ask those who heard me. Surely they know what I said."

When Jesus said this, one of the officials nearby struck him in the face. "Is this the way you answer the high priest?" he demanded.

"If I said something wrong," Jesus replied, "testify as to what is wrong. But if I spoke the truth, why did you strike me?" Then Annas sent him, still bound, to Caiaphas the high priest. John 18:20-24

30

THEY HATED HIM
WITHOUT A CAUSE

Having just been on my knees for your soul, and saying a special prayer for the souls of the Shepherds, hopefully your hearts are prepared to hear what all of HIS servants have been telling you in this book, and hopefully what David Wilkerson has to say next. If you stand faithfully with the love and forgiveness of Jesus against Satan's influence in the culture of the day, those against Jesus will hate you as they hated Him. Persevere and kneel at His feet daily, and He will give you peace, keep your eyes on Him. Now listen!

David Wilkerson June 15, 2009 Dearly Beloved: GOD HAS THE POWER, WISDOM, WILLINGNESS AND LOVE TO PRESERVE HIS BELOVED PEOPLE. If we are being asked to trust our lives to someone, we have to know that this someone has the power to keep us from all danger, threats and violence. Otherwise, our trust is in vain. Simply put, our God has to have the wisdom and power to guide us and countless multitudes through various crises and difficulties. And he must accomplish this guidance of his people in love. If you know the Lord at all, you know this is his character. He is almighty, infinitely wise, and a friend who sticks closer than a brother. Indeed, he is the very essence of love. Paul writes, *"I know whom I have believed, and am persuaded that he is able to keep that which I have committed unto him against that day"* (2 Timothy 1:12). Paul is saying, in essence, "I have put my life in the Lord's hands. And I am persuaded he won't embezzle my trust. He will faithfully keep his word to preserve me because he is both able and willing to do so. That has been my experience with the Lord."

Today, as storm clouds gather, our choice is clear: We can either resign our lives into the Lord's hands, or we can be responsible for keeping and preserving ourselves, a task that is impossible when God is shaking everything. The fact is, our peace and contentment always depend on our resignation into God's hands, no matter what our circumstance. The Psalmist writes, *"Delight thyself also in the Lord; and he shall give thee the desires of thine heart"* (Psalm 37:4). Your Father desires for you to be able to go about your daily business without fear or anxiety, totally trusting in his care. And your resignation to him has a very practical effect in your life. The more resigned you are to his care and keeping, the more indifferent you'll be to the conditions around you. If you are resigned to him, you won't constantly try to figure out the next step. You won't be scared by the frightful news swirling around you, or overwhelmed as you think about the days ahead, because you have entrusted your life, family and future into your Lord's safe and loving hands.

How worried or concerned do you think literal sheep are as they follow their shepherd into open pastures? They're not worried at all because they're totally resigned to his leading of them. Likewise, we are the sheep of Christ, who is our great Shepherd. Why should we ever be concerned, disquieted or worried about our lives and future? He knows perfectly how to protect and preserve his flock because he leads us in love.

Be warned: If you yield all to God, you'll be fiercely opposed by every power of darkness. Satan will erect mountains of frightful conditions before you, to try to drive you to unbelief. He'll flood you with doubts and fears that have never crossed your mind before. His strategy is to turn your focus onto "how bad things are going to get" rather than onto God's promises to keep you. We may see dangers on all sides, including a devil and his principalities who want to drown our faith in doubts. But we have a fiery guard of angels surrounding us and a God who is under oath to carry us through any disaster we may face. Do you want to face the coming storm with quiet confidence and peace of mind? Then die today to all your own ways and means of saving yourself and commit the keeping of your life wholly to God's care. He is your good, loving Shepherd who is faithful to see you through it all. A final word: Pray about everything. Ask the Holy Spirit to lead you in all your ways. Then rest. Let the peace of God fill your heart and mind. If God is with you, who can be against you? Your support of our ministry's many outreaches throughout the world is greatly appreciated. God bless you. In Christ, DAVID WILKERSON

"This cometh to pass, that the word might be fulfilled that is written in their law, They hated me without a cause" (John 15:25). Jesus said he came to seek out and save the lost. This was the same man who had power to subdue the very winds and waves. At any time Christ could have sent fire down from heaven

to destroy the wicked. Yet instead Jesus came as a humble servant. The Gospels tell us He listened patiently to people's heartbreaking cries. Multitudes pleaded with Christ to deliver them from their afflictions. And He met their needs: He healed the sick, opened blind eyes, unstopped deaf ears, loosed tied tongues, and made cripples to walk. Jesus set captives free from every form of bondage. He even raised their dead.

Even some nonbelievers agree: No one ever loved humankind more than Jesus did. He grieved over the multitudes before him, seeing them as lost sheep in need of a shepherd. The truth is, nobody in history should be more revered, respected and loved than Jesus Christ. He should be honored and highly esteemed by the entire world. He performed works of compassion for the people he met, he wept over the world's spiritual blindness and he poured out his life for all. In spite of the goodness Jesus performed, the world hated him without cause. There were ten thousand or more reasons for people to love Jesus and not one reason to hate him. The four Gospels portray him as kind, patient, long-suffering, full of tenderness, forgiving, willing that no person should perish. He is called a shepherd, a teacher, a brother, a light in darkness, a physician, an advocate, a reconciler. Jesus gave no cause whatsoever that he should be hated by anyone.

So, what did Christ do that He should be so despised, both in His own day and today? Simply put, the world hated Him because He came as a light to deliver them from darkness. Jesus declared Himself to be the light of the world: *"I am the light of the world: he that followeth me shall not walk in darkness, but shall have the light of life"* (John 8:12). Yet Christ also tells us, *"Every one that doeth evil hateth the light, neither cometh to the light, lest his deeds should be reproved"* (3:20). Christ's gospel includes the call to *"cast off the works of darkness, and...put on the armor of light"* (Romans 13:12).

Here is the reason the world has for hating Christ, both then and now. Jesus promised to deliver people from their chains of darkness. He pledged to set men everywhere free from all satanic power. However, what we Christians see as a holy gift of deliverance and liberty, the world sees as a form of bondage. They love their sins and have no desire to be free from them. "You call that freedom?" the nonbeliever asks. "No, here is freedom. We can do as we please with our bodies and minds. We declare ourselves free from all restrictions. We are already free — free from the bondage of the Bible, free from all sexual taboos, free to worship a god of our own choosing, including no god at all."

Simply put, the world loves the things of this world. The ungodly relish the pleasures of sin. Jesus said these prefer the darkness to the light. *"This is the condemnation [their reason for hating him], that light is come into the world, and men loved darkness rather than light, because their deeds were evil"* (John 3:19). Jesus warned his disciples clearly: *"Because I have chosen you out of this world, the world will hate you, just as they hated me."* Christ tells his followers, *"If ye were of the world, the world would love his own: but because ye are not of the world, but I have chosen you out of the world, therefore the world hateth you"* (John 15:19). Jesus adds in the same passage, *"If the world hate you, ye know that it hated me before it hated you"* (15:18). In short, if you are of Christ — if God chose you out of a worldly life to follow his Son, Jesus — you will never be loved or accepted by this world.

Why? Just as Christ said He is the light of the world, He declares us also to be the light of the world: *"Ye are the light of the world"* (Matthew 5:14). Think back for a moment to the time when you were born again in Christ. When you first saw the Light — that is, Jesus — you fell in love with Him. The things of the world you once loved now seemed despicable to you. And the holy things you had hated you now loved. You believed the Light. If Jesus brings such light, why is there so much rejection of him? Why so much mockery of His Word and ridicule of his church? Why does society go to such lengths to stamp out everything pertaining to Christ?

For years courts have tried to outlaw the very mention of His name. Why such abhorrence of Jesus and of those who hold to His Word as their moral compass? Think of how strange such hatred is. People don't usually hate those who love them. And true Christians exhibit love to the world. Those who walk wholeheartedly with Jesus are meek, friendly, forgiving, kind and even self-sacrificing. They respond to the human need all around them. Indeed, Christian groups are often the first responders in times of disaster. We bless the world both with our helping hands and with our prayers of comfort. Yet still we are hated.

We who call ourselves by the name of Christ are sons of peace, yet we are hated by the very world to which we offer help. This hatred toward followers of Jesus has to do with our mission as light bearers. As Christ's witnesses, we are called to a seemingly impossible task. Think about it: We are asking worldly people to give up those things that are absolutely dear to them. And we call them to a life that looks to their eyes like some form of slavery. What is heaven to us seems to them a kind of hell. Consider what we are called to do in witnessing to the world: We are asking people to forsake and turn away from the very sins they love. We are calling people to repent for having rejected the love and mercy of God, who demonstrated his love by giving up his Son on a cross. These people have struggled for years to silence the very conscience we appeal to. They don't want to hear some message about guilt. They've spent their lives trying to put to death any thought of a day of reckoning. We are called to tell sinful men and women that their own personal goodness — their moral uprightness and good works — cannot merit any right standing with God.

We are called to persuade self-made people that they must die to their own desires in order to give their lives for others. We are called to tell the worldly person that his integrity is as dirty rags in God's sight. In telling him this, we are taking from him his pearl of great price, the thing he worked so hard to obtain. And when we tell him no amount of self-earned righteousness can amount to salvation, he will despise us. Some say the preaching of the cross is too intolerant, as so-called "new evangelicals" seek accommodation for people's flesh. Many voices in the church today say Christians must accept and show a new kind of love. They're talking about a love in which biblical truth must bend with the times.

According to this gospel, no personal changes are necessary when one accepts Christ. Indeed, no repentance is needed. Rather, the goal in presenting this gospel is simple: to break down any barrier that could be considered a stumbling block to a person's acceptance of Christ. I ask you: Is it possible we have allowed the fullness of Christ's light to become partly darkened? Jesus warned about the danger that comes when our light becomes darkness. *"Take heed therefore that the light which is in you be not darkness"* (John 12:35). He's saying, in other words, "Let no part become dark."

Tell me, has our light darkened when polls show that 20 percent of evangelical youth accept same-sex marriage? Has our light become darkness when more and more Christians want to be loved and accepted by the world? According to Jesus, any desire for worldly acceptance causes our light to darken. I want to pose a question to all Christians reading this. Tell me, are you tired of the shame of the cross? Are you fed up with being mocked, dismissed, and seen as the off-scouring of the earth? Are you weary of being rejected and ridiculed? You can easily find acceptance. You can have the world call you friend, associate with you, admire you, even love the kind of gospel you preach.

How? It happens when you allow the ways of the world to seep into your soul. You cast off the reproach of Christ, convincing yourself you can mix with darkness and still be a light to the world. No, it does not work! If you succumb to such friendship with the world, your light will become darkness.

Jesus describes the process: *"If thine eye be evil, thy whole body shall be full of darkness. If therefore the light that is in thee be darkness, how great is that darkness!"* (Matthew 6:23). Such is the condition of your soul when something of the world has taken hold. At the Last Supper, Christ warned his disciples, *"Some of you will be killed, some will be imprisoned, and all will be persecuted."* At this point, Jesus gave the disciples a word of direction. It was meant to teach them how to reach their generation after he was gone. He told them, *"A new commandment I give unto you"* (John 13:34).

This new commandment was not about methods of evangelism. Jesus had already told them they were to go into the entire world preaching his gospel. He had also instructed them they would need the Holy Ghost to fulfill that command. Now he was giving them a totally different commandment, one they hadn't heard before. Jesus told these men plainly: "If you will obey this new commandment, all men will know who you are. It will cause them to know exactly where you stand. They may hate you, call you a fanatic, accuse you of bigotry. They may kick you out of their synagogues. But they will see and know that you are mine." What was this new commandment? Jesus told them, *"A new commandment I give unto you, That ye love one another; as I have loved you, that ye also love one another"* (13:34).

This commandment is not an option but is directed to every follower of Christ. This one commandment is where all evangelistic efforts begin. Yes, we are to feed the poor, do many good works and preach Christ boldly. But if we are to penetrate the "gross darkness" that increasingly covers the world, we need to lay hold of this new commandment. Through it, we will be totally identified as being "of the light." *"By this shall all men know that ye are my disciples, if ye have love one to another"* (John 13:35). Our love for one another in the church must not be merely in word but demonstrated in deed. Only love in action will get the attention of a lost generation. It will cause the world to recognize this is the same love that Jesus has toward his people. This love is the only way to penetrate the darkness. And it is our only response to the world's hatred. *"Love one another; as I have loved you"* (13:34).

We don't need a book or a list to show us how to love as Christ loved us. I can sum it all up in one sentence: It means laying down your life for those of like faith. In fact, I can name it in a single word: martyrdom. *"Greater love hath no man than this, that a man lay down his life for his friends"* (15:13). The author of Hebrews tells us, *"Others were tortured, not accepting deliverance"* (Hebrews 11:35, my italics). When this testimony was recorded, the church of Jesus Christ was still mostly an underground movement. The persecutors who tormented these Christians demanded to know, "Who are your pastors? Where do you meet? Tell us the names of the people you worship with." But these believers loved their brethren even as Christ had loved them. So they suffered for the sake of their fellow saints, to the point they laid down their very lives for them. *"They were stoned, they were sawn asunder...were slain with the sword"* (Hebrews 11:37).

Let me tell you what I know about modern-day martyrs. I know some of their names. These people are destitute, afflicted, tormented. Many endure torment of mind, soul and body on a daily basis. Some suffer such pain and anguish they would welcome death. These precious believers are laying down their lives every day by keeping faith in their time of great anguish and testing. Surviving, they go on, holding onto faith one day at a time.

We who live in free nations also "lay down our lives" in a sense. It happens each time we trust God through another day, praising him in our adversities. All the while, many eyes are watching us. Nonbelievers who have heard us testify of God's keeping power examine our actions closely. And baby believers monitor our faith as they struggle through their own doubts. The fact is, no other kind of love gets the attention of "all men" as does sacrificial love for our brethren.

Why is this "new commandment" from Jesus so important today? It is urgently important because the Holy Spirit has brought to our generation a great sense of need. Consider: Why is drinking and alcoholism on the rise? Why are increasing numbers of people turning to drugs? Why are there so many suicides? The answer is simple: People everywhere are hurting. There is "sin sickness" all over the world, with multitudes facing empty days and anguished nights. They find so little to trust in. To whom can they turn? Where will they find someone who can show them hope? Where is there a source of real compassion, someone who himself has endured pain and suffering? The hurting and bewildered of the world aren't going to turn to people who question their own faith. They won't seek out a people who think God has placed more on them than they can bear. Of course, it's true that all believers have their "crying times." Even the godliest Christian can be overwhelmed by sorrows and trials. For many saints, personal pain has grown so powerful they have succumbed to weariness, feeling utterly helpless. Yet amid their sorrows, they continue to cry out to the Lord. In their grief, they lay hold of the Father's comforting promises. And daily they rise up again and fight on with renewed faith.

These believers simply do not quit. They trust the Holy Spirit to keep their light of faith burning, for Christ's sake and for the sake of his church. Dear saint, this is where true love begins: with laying down our dreams, hopes and plans, to share in the sufferings of Christ and yield willingly to our cross. That is the love all men can see. *"By this shall all men know that ye are my disciples"* (John 13:35).

David Wilkerson is one that has been faithful to Jesus, please receive a blessing by reading his commentaries and watching his videos, they will inspire and if you pray, give you courage in these urgent times, Shepherds listen up! Dr. Gregory Thompson

I came to know another warrior for the Lord, one that understands the times, Fr. Donnelly gets past the rhetoric because of the lives and souls of the children being at risk, he stands up as a Shepherd and others desiring to be a true Shepherd should listen intently to the words that drive Fr. Donnelly, "Ora et age" (Pray and act) . Jesus taught us to do just that, it was Jesus the Master, Jesus the true Shepherd, Jesus the true Teacher, yes kneel down and pray to cover all actions, and then get up with the power of the Holy Spirit and go to the cross. If you have a Shepherd that teaches anything other than what Jesus teaches, run from them as fast as you can. *"Come, all you beasts of the field, come and devour, all you beasts of the forest! Israel's (America's) watchmen are blind, they all lack knowledge; they are all dumb dogs, they cannot bark; they lie around and dream, they love to sleep. They are dogs with mighty appetites; they never have enough. They are shepherds who lack understanding; they all turn to their own way, each seeks his own gain. "Come," each one cries, "let me get wine! Let us drink our fill of beer! And tomorrow will be like today, or even far better"* (Isaiah 56: 9-12).

31

WOE TO SELF SERVING DISOBEDIENCE

"Woe to the worthless shepherd, who deserts the flock! May the sword strike his arm and his right eye! May his arm be completely withered, his right eye totally blinded" (Zechariah 11:16,17)!

The Shepherd that does not trust in God has a tough job that can cause much pain to himself and to those in his flock. When they disobey God they put the lives and souls of others at risk, and risk a higher condemnation from God. He will cast out of His sight, any unrepentant Shepherd that serves himself. Pray that such men change their heart and ways before they do harm to God's children and put themselves at risk. Listen to God's word speaking to the Shepherds.

Then Jesus said to the crowds and to his disciples: "The teachers of the law and the Pharisees sit in Moses' seat. So you must obey them and do everything they tell you. But do not do what they do, for they do not practice what they preach. They tie up heavy loads and put them on men's shoulders, but they themselves are not willing to lift a finger to move them.

"Everything they do is done for men to see: They make their phylacteries wide and the tassels on their garments long; they love the place of honor at banquets and the most important seats in the synagogues; they love to be greeted in the marketplaces and to have men call them 'Rabbi.'

"But you are not to be called 'Rabbi,' for you have only one Master and you are all brothers. And do not call anyone on earth 'father,' for you have one Father, and he is in heaven. Nor are you to be called 'teacher,' for you have one Teacher, the Christ. The greatest among you will be your servant. For whoever exalts himself will be humbled, and whoever humbles himself will be exalted.

"Woe to you, teachers of the law and Pharisees, you hypocrites! You shut the kingdom of heaven in men's faces. You yourselves do not enter, nor will you let those enter who are trying to.

"Woe to you, teachers of the law and Pharisees, you hypocrites! You travel over land and sea to win a single convert, and when he becomes one, you make him twice as much a son of hell as you are.

"Woe to you, blind guides! You say, 'If anyone swears by the temple, it means nothing; but if anyone swears by the gold of the temple, he is bound by his oath.' You blind fools! Which is greater: the gold, or the temple that makes the gold sacred? You also say, 'If anyone swears by the altar, it means nothing; but if anyone swears by the gift on it, he is bound by his oath.' You blind men! Which is greater: the gift, or the altar that makes the gift sacred? Therefore, he who swears by the altar swears by it and by everything on it. And he who swears by the temple swears by it and by the one who dwells in it. And he who swears by heaven swears by God's throne and by the one who sits on it.

"Woe to you, teachers of the law and Pharisees, you hypocrites! You give a tenth of your spices—mint, dill and cummin. But you have neglected the more important matters of the law—justice, mercy and faithfulness. You should have practiced the latter, without neglecting the former. You blind guides! You strain out a gnat but swallow a camel.

"Woe to you, teachers of the law and Pharisees, you hypocrites! You clean the outside of the cup and dish, but inside they are full of greed and self-indulgence. Blind Pharisee! First clean the inside of the cup and dish, and then the outside also will be clean.

"Woe to you, teachers of the law and Pharisees, you hypocrites! You are like whitewashed tombs, which look beautiful on the outside but on the inside are full of dead men's bones and everything unclean. In the same way, on the outside you appear to people as righteous but on the inside you are full of hypocrisy and wickedness.

"Woe to you, teachers of the law and Pharisees, you hypocrites! You build tombs for the prophets and decorate the graves of the righteous. And you say, 'If we had lived in the days of our forefathers, we would not have taken part with them in shedding the blood of the prophets.' So you testify against yourselves that you are the descendants of those who murdered the prophets. Fill up, then, the measure of the sin of your forefathers!

"You snakes! You brood of vipers! How will you escape being condemned to hell? Therefore I am sending you prophets and wise men and teachers. Some of them you will kill and crucify; others you will flog in your synagogues and pursue from town to town. And so upon you will come all the righteous blood that has been shed on earth, from the blood of righteous Abel to the blood of

Zechariah son of Berekiah, whom you murdered between the temple and the altar. I tell you the truth, all this will come upon this generation.

"O Jerusalem, Jerusalem, you who kill the prophets and stone those sent to you, how often I have longed to gather your children together, as a hen gathers her chicks under her wings, but you were not willing. Look, your house is left to you desolate. For I tell you, you will not see me *again until you say, 'Blessed is he who comes in the name of the Lord'" (Matthew 23).*

Please do not lie to yourself by turning your eyes away from any of these warnings that you own, don't rationalize your guilt away, as you know that you were in the crowd in some way, that was crying "Crucify him! Crucify him! You Shepherds, I plead with you to turn your heart to God and His ways. Put away your pride, and disobedience, and silence, and greed and fear that continues to allow the children to be murdered while you are comfortable on your pillows, that continues to put HIS children's souls at risk as you hide behind the pulpit with a different Christ than the one given to the saints. With the love of Christ I pray and ask God to put you to your knees and break your strongholds that keep you from denying yourself, and that keep you from giving your life for the sheep in your care.

Shepherds you should know that Jesus wishes that none would perish, yet some of you put yourself in a position Judas was in at the Last Supper when Jesus replied, *"The one who has dipped his hand into the bowl with me will betray me. The Son of Man will go just as it is written about him. But woe to that man who betrays the Son of Man! It would be better for him if he had not been born." Then Judas (Shepherd pray that your name is not written here because of your blindness), the one who would betray him, said, "Surely not I, Rabbi?" Jesus answered, "Yes, it is you" (Matthew 26:23-25).*

Shepherd, priest, pastor, elder, ministry leader, it is important for you to read what another Apostle says and hear the words of Christ again, so that you can go to your knees and ask forgiveness for your sins you had an active part in and for your sins of omission.

Burn this into your heart now, so that you do not burn later: *"The Son of Man will go just as it is written about him. But woe to that man who betrays the Son of Man! It would be better for him if he had not been born" (Mark 14:21).*

Shepherds, (Notre Dame and other Christian schools, *"Your attitude should be the same as that of Christ Jesus: Who, being in very nature God, did not consider equality with God something to be grasped, but made himself nothing, taking the very nature of a servant, being made in human likeness. And being found in appearance as a man, he humbled himself and became obedient to death— even death on a cross! Therefore God exalted him to the highest place and gave him the name that is above every name, that at the name of Jesus every knee should bow, in heaven and on earth and under the earth, and every tongue confess that Jesus Christ is Lord, to the glory of God the Father. (2 Cor. 2:5-11).*

Pastor Ernie Sanders tries to imitate the One True Shepherd. He does not take a salary, feeds the poor and helps the less fortunate, will not register his church with the state for them to control in any way, visits and ministers to men on death row, has been used by God to save many babies and mothers from abortion, and continues to host What's Right What's Left Radio for over 35 years with an identity of "Voice of the Christian Resistance." Pray for him to stay in the will of God, and send your prayers, love, and support for his ministry.

Then Jesus said to his disciples, *"If anyone would come after me, he must deny himself and take up his cross and follow me. For whoever wants to save his life will lose it, but whoever loses his life for me will find it. What good will it be for a man if he gains the whole world, yet forfeits his soul? Or what can a man give in exchange for his soul? For the Son of Man is going to come in his Father's glory with his angels, and then he will reward each person according to what he has done"* (Matt 16). To know what to do it is so important that we go to the only one with the answer, God Himself, in the person of Jesus Christ, answers this question all of us search for. This question is given great insight by Pope John Paul II in this passage from his book *"The Splendor of Truth."*

32

"TEACHER WHAT GOOD MUST I DO...?"

"Then someone came to him…". In the young man, whom Matthew's Gospel does not name, we can recognize every person who, consciously or not, approaches Christ the Redeemer of man and questions him about morality. For the young man, the question is not so much about rules to be followed, but about the full meaning of life. This is in fact the aspiration at the heart of every human decision and action, the quiet searching and interior prompting which sets freedom in motion. This question is ultimately an appeal to the absolute Good which attracts us and beckons us; it is the echo of a call from God who is the origin and goal of man's life. Precisely in this perspective the Second Vatican Council called for a renewal of moral theology, so that its teaching would display the lofty vocation which the faithful have received in Christ, the only response fully capable of satisfying the desire of the human heart.

In order to make this "encounter" with Christ possible, God willed His Church. Indeed, the Church "wishes to serve this single end: that each person may be able to find Christ, in order that Christ may walk with each person the path of life."

"Teacher, what good must I do to have eternal life?" The question which the rich young man puts to Jesus of Nazareth is one which rises from the depths of his heart. It is an essential and unavoidable question for the life of every man, for it is about the moral good which must be done, and about eternal life. The young man sensed that there was a connection between moral good and the fulfillment of his own destiny. He was a devout Israelite, raised as it were in the shadow of the Low of the Lord. If he asked Jesus this question, we can presume that it was not because he was ignorant of the answer contained in the Law. It is more likely that the attractiveness of the person of Jesus had prompted within him new questions about moral good. He felt the need to draw near to the One who had begun preaching with this new and decisive proclamation: *"The time is fulfilled, and the Kingdom of God is at hand; repent, and believe in the Gospel"* (Mark 1:15).

People today need to turn to Christ once again in order to receive from him the answer to their questions about what is good and what is evil. Christ is the Teacher, the Risen One who has life in himself and who is always present in his Church and in the world. It is he who opens up to the faithful the book of the Scriptures and, by fully revealing the Father's will, teaches the truth about moral action. At the source and summit of the economy of salvation, as the Alpha and the Omega of human history (Rev 1:8; 21:6; 22:13), Christ sheds light on man's condition and his integral vocation. Consequently, "the man who wishes to understand himself thoroughly—and not just in accordance with immediate, partial, and often superficial, and even illusory standards and measures of his being—must with his unrest, uncertainty and even his weakness and sinfulness, with his life and death, draw near to Christ. He must, so to speak, enter HIM with all his own self; he must 'appropriate' and assimilate the whole of the reality of the Incarnation and Redemption in order to find himself. If this profound process takes place within him, he then bears fruit not only of adoration of God but also of deeper wonder at himself."

If we therefore wish to go to the heart of the Gospel's moral teaching and grasp its profound and unchanging content, we must carefully inquire into the meaning of the question asked by the rich young man in the Gospel and, even more, the meaning of Jesus' reply, allowing ourselves to be guided by HIM. Jesus, as a patient and sensitive teacher, answers the young man by taking him, as it were, by the hand, and leading him step by step to the full truth.

Thank you Pope John Paul II, my heart cries out for a time we will again have Shepherds that lead us step by step to the full truth, with no ulterior motives, and with Holy Spirit strength and boldness, because they love us enough to want us in heaven for eternity.

33

THE COUNTERFEIT GOSPEL IS REAL!

There is a considerable amount of scripture warning us about religious deception and the ministers of it. There are obvious phony religions such as Islam, Buddhism, Hinduism, Scientology, and a host of others. However, in the midst of this is a counterfeit of Christianity, which is just as damning as the false religions I mentioned.

The Prophets of the Old Testament, Jesus and the Apostles in the New Testament each addressed this most serious subject, and so should anyone else led by the Holy Spirit. Yet, in our day, there seems to be a shortage of teaching about this topic.

The Word and Discernment

Exposing bogus religion and false teachings is a Biblical mandate to every Christian including ministers. The Book of Jude warns Christians to *"earnestly contend* [fight] *for the Faith."* We are to stand up for the true faith. This is not a passive action and it requires us to be focused and energized by the Holy Spirit.

We have this warning from Jude because there are those who use the Bible to mislead people into false doctrines and half-truths that undermine the true faith. This little epistle of Jude speaks about false Apostles who *"crept in unawares* [secretly]." Where did they creep? They crept into the true church, and the people were unaware of it.

The book of Titus is a guide for ministers called of God. As ministers of righteousness, we should be blameless stewards of God, holding fast to His word. Scripture commands us to use sound doctrine to expose the vain talkers and deceivers who mislead entire households by teaching things forbidden, for ill-gotten money. Ministers are instructed to rebuke them sharply with a purpose of making them sound in the faith.

A counterfeit gospel looks like the real thing, and it takes the word of God and discernment from the Holy Spirit to comprehend the difference. There are many aspects and people involved in spurious gospel teachings, and most who are caught up in this do not even realize it—however Satan is behind it all.

Satan attempts to lure people away from the solid truth of scripture. He tried it with Jesus, but failed in his attempt to twist the truth of God. This was an old trick he used on Adam and Eve and they fell for it, and he still uses it today. Satan is a seducer! I Timothy 4:1, warns Christians about "*seducing spirits, and doctrines of devils.*" Because of many false prophets, I John 4 tells us not to believe "*every spirit, but to try the spirits whether they are of God...*"

The Apostle Paul addressed the counterfeit of Christianity in 2 Corinthians 11:4 when he warned us about another Jesus, another spirit, and another gospel. Verses 14 and 15 tell us, "*Satan himself is transformed into an angel of light. Therefore, it is no great thing if his ministers also be transformed as the ministers of righteousness.*" He was referring to false apostles pretending to be apostles of Christ, who in reality were not sent by God.

The Lord intended for Christians, in all generations, to realize that He has not called everyone who teaches and preaches from the Bible! As I have stated, Christians need discernment, from the Holy Spirit, to spot preachers who teach false doctrines. This is something every Christian should know. However, some have no idea this is in the Bible. When was the last time you heard a message on this subject? I hope is has not been long.

None of us are above being fooled. If we are not grounded in scripture and in touch with our Lord through prayer, and open to the discernment of the Holy Spirit, we can be duped by an imitation gospel.

I believe there are people who go to church and have no idea whether they are following God or the devil. If we seek the Lord, our Heavenly Father will show us who our Father really is—the devil or God! He will show that which is false and that which is real.

In John 8, Jesus told the Jewish religious leaders that their father was the devil. They had plenty of religion, but their heart was wrong. They tithed, prayed, studied Scripture and were in the Temple at the appointed times—however, they had no idea their religion was false and inspired by Satan. He has a supernatural power and he uses it to deceive people in the church. A growing number of people, who say they are Christian, do not even believe the devil is real.

The devil attempts to deceive people into following him rather than God. Isaiah 14 tells us that the devil views himself as being above God. He said,

"I will be like the most High." To be *like* something is not the same as *being* something. He is a counterfeit and uses any minister possible to promote his false teachings or a false religion.

In 2 Timothy 3, the Apostle Paul speaks to false Christianity when he describes the perilous last days. I believe this is speaking of the days we are living in. In verses 5 and 6, he tells us that people will have *"a form of godliness,"* and to *"turn away"* from it. A form of something can look like the real thing, like counterfeit money, which is often difficult to detect. We are to ditch any false teaching, even if our favorite preacher promotes it.

The subject of a "form of godliness" continues in verse 13, as the apostle writes, *"But evil men and seducers will wax worse and worse, deceiving and being deceived."* As I have stated, only discernment from the Holy Spirit can reveal these things to us.

Some people are prime victims of false doctrines and false teachers. They love the feel good, compromised sugarcoated gospel, which may sound correct, but in reality, it does not bring them to a proper repentance, self-denial or a truthful submission to Jesus Christ. Their belief is in vain. They may go to church, worship and praise God, study the Bible, and may even call Jesus Lord, but Jesus does not know them!

Jesus Must Be the Object of Our Faith

In Matthew 7:15, Jesus warns us about false prophets, and their fruit. In verses 21-23 He warns us that, *"Not everyone that saith unto me, 'Lord, Lord,' shall enter into the kingdom of heaven; but he that doeth the will of my Father which is in heaven. Many will say to me on that day, 'Lord, Lord, have we not prophesied in Thy name, and in Thy name have cast out devils? And in Thy name done many wonderful works?' Then will I profess unto them, I never knew you: depart from me, ye that work iniquity."*

These are shocking words spoken by our Lord. It does not matter what we say or do unless Jesus truly becomes our Lord through repentance and a heartfelt belief of His Gospel. The Holy Spirit bears witness with us whether or not we are a true believer.

The Apostle Paul says this in 2 Corinthians 13, *"Examine yourselves, whether ye be in the faith; prove your own selves. Know ye not your own selves, how that Jesus Christ is in you, except ye be reprobates?"*

Nice sounding words mean nothing if they come from a heart far from the Lord. An example of this is the religious scribes and Pharisees in Matthew 15:7-9. Jesus called them hypocrites who drew close to Him with their mouth, and honored Him with their lips; but their heart was far from Him and they taught doctrines and commandments of men. Their words were right, but their worship was wrong.

In spite of how great the message may sound, if it takes us away from the cross of Christ and complete faith in what Jesus did there, it is not the true Gospel! Jesus, and obedience to Him, must be the object of our Faith. To focus on our human ability and will power frustrates [voids] the grace of God, yet many people trust in themselves.

Counterfeit Ministry

Much of evangelical America is big business today. Christ is preached and professed from multitudes of pulpits, however, He is denied in various ways! There are too many churches where Jesus is not permitted to be the head of the church. These places are led by ministers anointed with the spirit of the world rather than God's Holy Spirit. An alarming number of churches exist, today, because their leaders have learned to use worldly business techniques to attract a crowd.

Some ministers are drunk with the lust for fame or power and they compromise to get it. Others love money and compromise the message because they are afraid of losing that "good giver."

Still others work to build large ministries to feed their ego. Some of them are like corporate CEO's who use business techniques to build crowds— sometimes even into huge mega-churches. There is lots of glitz and glamour with few or no true conversions. Compromising the word of God to please people is the order of the day in a growing number of churches. There is a multitude of ungodly motives in our pulpits today and those who support this foolishness need to wake up!

Many churches select a pastor based on education, success at another church; or how charming they are! Most pulpit committees take a carnal approach in selecting a pastor. They rarely shut themselves up with God for prayer and direction, because they want that good-looking resume. What do they get?

They get the spirit of the world. Social clubs with prayer-less ministers who refuse to seek the Lord for guidance in their preaching or any aspect of the church. They get preachers who take polls in the community to see what people want to hear.

They get ministers who constantly scan the Internet for clever sermon ideas or they will preach something from their favorite TV preacher. Much of the time, the church gets deceptive false doctrines and a counterfeit faith.

There is no anointing from the Holy Spirit in many of our churches today. However, the spirit of the world is rampant, and many people love to have it so!

As a result, the music and message in many churches and media ministries, has become so watered down, it offends no one. It is a counterfeit gospel of sugarcoated, up-lifting messages adapted to fit the sinful needs of the fallen sinful nature of mankind. The clever messages in most churches entertain; promote a positive mental attitude, worldly success, how to get rich, and many other flesh pleasing topics. It's the wisdom of man and sounds good to the self-centered sin nature, but it is all bogus!

"And I, brethren, when I came to you, came not with excellency of speech or of wisdom, declaring unto you the testimony of God. For I determined not to know any thing among you, save Jesus Christ, and him crucified. And I was with you in weakness, and in fear, and in much trembling. And my speech and my preaching was not with enticing words of man's wisdom, but in demonstration of the Spirit and of power: That your faith should not stand in the wisdom of men, but in the power of God. Howbeit we speak wisdom among them that are perfect: yet not the wisdom of this world, nor of the princes of this world, that come to naught:" That is an example of how we are to preach, given to us by the Apostle Paul in II Corinthians 2:1-5.

The Name Christian is tossed Around a Lot

Have you noticed? We have so-called Christian ventriloquists, Christian magicians, Christian comedians, Christian tattoos, Christian nightclubs, Christian youth centers full of rebellion and the spirit of the world. Were these methods used to reach the world when the church began in the books of Acts? The answer is no!

There are many Christian movements today. God's people need Holy Spirit discernment to know the ones sent by God, and the ones that are of the devil! Recently, *Newsweek* magazine reported about a new Christian men's movement, called the GodMen. Their story featured a gathering of men in a Nashville warehouse.

There were strobe lights and rebellious Christian rock music blaring through thumping speakers. A huge video screen showed people doing stupid stunts. Then it quieted down a little when a Christian comedian took the stage and shouted, "Are you ready to be a man? Are you ready to kick a_ _?" The article said the crowd loved it.

Deceived preachers need to repent and ditch the foolishness we see so much of today, and preach the word of God without fear!

2 Timothy 4:1-4 is a charge, from the Apostle Paul to Timothy and to every minister the Lord would call thereafter. It says, *"Preach the word; be instant in season, out of season; reprove; rebuke, exhort with all longsuffering and doctrine. For the time will come when they will not endure sound doctrine; but after their own lust shall they heap to themselves teachers, having itching ears; and they shall turn away their ears from the truth, and shall be turned unto fables."*

Preaching the entire word of God exposes sin, which often does not set well with certain individuals. However, we are to do so even in the face of rejection. We are not to compromise the doctrines of scripture to comfort those who have ears that itch to hear fleshly things that stroke their egos and make them feel good.

All Scripture is given by inspiration of God for doctrine, for reproof, for correction, and for instruction in righteousness. A person must have the will to let the word work in their heart. Many refuse it and like our text says, turn away from the truth to lies.

While words proclaim the cross of Christ in many churches, actions proclaim something different—the cross is not the object of the faith and Jesus is not the way. Many Christians have left their first love, Jesus! Like wolves in sheep's clothing, predators in the pulpit are preying on lukewarm sheep in the pews. The blind are leading the blind.

It's not common to attend church and see folks weeping and begging God for forgiveness of their sins. There is no pleading with God to create a clean heart and a right spirit within them.

The Holy Spirit is whispering to the church to come out of the world, repent and return to their first love. However, heartfelt cries of repentance are rare in comparison to the lust for self-indulgence. Growing numbers of churches have no tears at the altar, but they are saturated with the spirit of the world and proud flesh.

Revival!

I hope you are praying for revival. Our churches need the touch of God—a Heaven sent, pride busting, soul trembling, hell shaking revival! One that produces broken spirits and contrite hearts—the real sacrifices of God!

R.L. is a pastor/evangelist and president of R.L. Beasley Ministries, based in Joplin, Missouri. He conducts "Crusades for Christ Revivals;" and is the editor of the "Beacon," a monthly ministry and news publication. He is in demand as a speaker for Christian conferences and is the former state director for the American Family Association of Missouri. R.L. lives in Joplin with his wife Marilyn.

For more information: Website: www. rlbeasleyministries.com Address: P.O. Box 2862 * Joplin, MO 64803-2862 * Phone: 417-781-5059. Email: rlbeasley@att.net

R.L. is a warrior servant for Jesus, and has had many times been in a position to tell the truth, which does not always get you invited back. Many people want a feel good message that, many times, does not conform to the Absolute Truth. Like Pastor R.L. Beasley, Pastor Bill Dunfee, gives a needed message to convict both the pulpit and the pew.   Pray again that the Holy Spirit will protect you from being counterfeit or willfully ignorant. The Sheep depend on your vigilance to protect them from the wolves, woe to those that decide to be ignorant, read James 4:17 again, and repent, pray, and then pick up your cross and follow Christ.

34

WILLFUL IGNORANCE

John 4:29-35 this is where Jesus ministers to a woman caught in Adultery. Jesus changes her life and she goes and tells others.

Jesus says, "Don't say the harvest is yet to come." Jesus says "just lift up your eyes that you may see the harvest." Now that still applies to us today. Don't you think so? I want you to think about it for just a second. When was the last time you saw the harvest? When was the last time you lifted up your eyes to see the harvest that is before us? Now I would say that if you're in someone's shoes and you go to a prison and minister, you will see the harvest. If you go to the abortion mills you see the harvest If you are involved in the street ministries, you see the harvest. I pray that everyone is able to see the harvest, but I'm afraid we have become so involved in life we have made it extremely difficult to see the harvest. And if we do see, the vision we have is tainted. That which we see is blurred, and the reason it is blurred is because when we watch the news or read the newspaper or we listen to the radio, all we hear is the hopelessness of our times.

Murder, stealing, killing, you name it. You read the newspapers and what is spot lighted? Terrorism and evil is always in the spot light. So you listen to the radio and again what is spot lighted? It's the evil. So what happens when we lift up our eyes and we are capable of seeing the harvest; we see it but we just don't believe it. Why? Because the people are just so mean and evil that they will never hear or come. We have been so tainted with the evil that surrounds us that we get to the point in our lives that we know the harvest is plentiful but we don't believe that it's possible to bring it in, because we're in a hopeless situation.

Recently, I was outside the Foxhole (a strip joint we were trying to close down), and I thought to myself, "this is never going to end." Evil is going to prevail. Evil is going to triumph. I was thinking, where does it all end? It got to the point where you would see people pull in, and I would see them and want to say, "Just get away from me." I wouldn't say that to their face, but that was the attitude I had in my heart. Why? I saw the harvest, but I just couldn't believe that there could be a harvest. Why? It was because of what I saw. Flip makes the statement, "you serve the God that you see." What we see determines how we'll behave, how we'll respond and we cannot see with the spiritual eye beyond that which is natural. Now we are in trouble aren't we?

If we cannot see with our spiritual eye, what is beyond our natural eye. If all we do is look at the natural in the natural realm. We'll throw up our hands, we'll throw in the towel, we'll retreat, we will just give up. We will go through the motions, but down inside we won't believe there will be a harvest, because we are looking at how things are naturally.

Now Jesus said to the disciples, "don't pray for the harvest, don't look for the harvest down the road, lift up your eyes and see it." See it with your spiritual eye.

We need to have our vision transformed? I believe it's essential and it's critical. But the question is, "how can you have your vision transformed so you can literally see the harvest." So

Jesus makes it very clear in the passages of Scripture. You need to have your vision restored, because you see Jesus looks at the church and I dare say he looks at us and what he sees is a complacent, lukewarm, compromising people. That is what He sees. When he looks at us, the church in America, who has all kinds of stuff, who say they are rich, who have these mega, fortresses, who have bank accounts and who have big attendances, Jesus looks at us and He says, "I would rather that you be hot or I'd rather that you be cold and since you're neither, I'm going to spit you out.

Now how does Christ see the church? Well how do we know that we can classify as a lukewarm people, Christians? Well let's talk about the harvest. Do you see it? Are we bringing it in? What excites us? What ignites us? Where is our passion, our zeal? What drives us and motivates us? Is it God and His Word, the things of the Lord? Is it the Holy Spirit at work in us? What is it that gets us up in the morning and gets us going? Then you would agree with me that we need to see ourselves as Jesus sees us. He said, the very first step to a transformed vision is a restored vision. It's time to get your eye sight back. It's time to get your eyes sight back. See the enemy to the true reality, is the natural reality. Natural reality obscures true reality.

Now what do I mean by that? Natural reality says there is hope. Natural reality says this I've tried and I've tried and I've shared and I've shared. That is what natural reality says, isn't it? True reality is what? Faith in God's word.

True reality is this, that you are more than conquerors through Jesus Christ our Lord. True reality is this, that it is not in vain. True reality is this, you are doing a good thing and don't give up. You are on the brink if we could just hear God.

But it's hard to focus on the truth. We know we're not running in vain. We know we are more than conquerors. Isn't that the truth?

If God is for us, who can be against us, isn't that the truth? No weapons that could form against you could ever prosper because you dwell under the shadow of the Most HIGH, isn't that the truth? Isn't it true that healing is the children's bread? Isn't that the truth? I have never seen the righteous begging for bread. True reality; that's the way God sees it. He says lift up your eyes and see what I see and have your vision restored.

Sometimes we have to admit it, we have to step back and get an eye exam and say, "you know what God, I have lost my heart, I have lost my focus, I have lost my sight, I have become discouraged, I have become complacent, I am giving up." Would you agree with that? (Authors note: Stop right now, and get to your knees and pray for the Shepherds to be protected from evil, that they receive courage, that the scales come off of their eyes, and that they again can lead and protect the sheep.) Sometimes we have to do that.

I have come to this conclusion, if God sees value in us standing up there at any place where evil exists and sharing the gospel until He comes, than I guess we need to stand there until He comes again. The truth of the matter is that we are affective. The truth of the matter there are some things happening, the truth of the matter is God is at work. The truth of the matter is my father is getting saved, that is the truth. The truth of the matter is there will be people that will be blessed by our sacrifice as Christians.

1. We have to see ourselves right now for who we are and where we are and if there is a luke warmness or complacency or if we have succumbed to an element of compromise, "Oh I'd never compromise," even as we sometimes compromise in a way we don't call compromising. We say, "I know I'm supposed to be doing this but I just don't see the value in it. So I'll stop doing it until a later date." That is compromise. Compromise is disobedience. In order to have transformed vision, you've got to have restored vision.

Now there will come a time when I've got to do step number 2 and that is go get me some council from an eye doctor. He will restore my vision if it's possible and I believe it is.

2. We must receive the council of Jesus. Jesus said to the Laodacians, I know your works, I know who you are, I know what you think of yourselves, I know everything about you. You think you're rich, you think you've got it altogether, and then He says, "I counsel thee to buy gold tried in the fire that thou may be rich. Do you see that? Do you see what Jesus is telling them? I counsel thee to buy gold tried by fire, that you may be rich, so how do we become rich? How do we become rich in Christ Jesus? We've got to go through the fire. The Lord steps in and He says, "because I see you for who you are, and you've not come to the point of believing who you are, I counsel you to buy gold tried by the fire, that you may be rich. So in order to be rich in Christ Jesus we have to be tried by fire and come out on the other end with our faith still planted in Christ. And the only way you can go through the fire is to go through some tough times. Some tough experiences, where all of life seems to be against you. Then it tells you how good your vision really is.

Do you have natural sight or the true sight, the spiritual sight? Are you able to see thru and beyond to know that God is working in the midst of this thing. He says to be tried in the fire. Then He goes on and says, my other advice to you is this, that thou may be clothed in white raiment, that the shame of thy nakedness, the Lord looks and says, I see a bunch of naked people." What's He mean by that? You are running around in your own self righteousness. See when He's talking about buying white raiment, He's talking about putting on righteousness. Who's righteousness? His! You see if we've not been redeemed and restored in Christ Jesus and walking in Christ Jesus, if we are walking in our own flesh and our own natural ambitions and strengths and desire, He says, "you are naked." Oh, you think that you are strutting your stuff, you think you're the best dressed in church, but you are naked.

First, get tested in fire. Second, put on some clothes.

It starts by admitting who and what we are, and asking Jesus for some white raiment, and then our shame will be covered up. Then He says, anoint your eyes with eye salve that you might see. Anoint your eyes, allow the Holy Spirit to anoint you to the point where you are able to spiritually see, able to discern, able to know that no longer do you trust in the natural, in the things that we put our confidence in, but see it as it is, lift up your eyes, because it's here right in front of you. Once you receive this counseling, what you need to do next is come up higher.

Now the throne of God is the seat of authority and of power, and victory, to those who will receive their vision restored and receive counsel from ME, they will be invited to come up and sit by my throne. We need to get to the point in our lives where we are coming up. Get into that position that Christ has called us. In John 4:1, what did Jesus first say to John? He just shared with John what was happening with the churches in Asia Miner. He just showed him what was happening in the church of the Laodiceans, and Jesus said to the Christians of Laodicea, be of me, trust in me, receive counsel of me, and if you will do that, you will get to come up higher. Then He said, John, come up here. That is where we need to live our lives? Not down here but up there. He said, John come up here I have a spiritual vantage point for you.

When you want to see far, where do you go? You go up higher. You get above the obstacles. I like to deer hunt from a tree stand, why? It gives me the advantage, I can see better, I can see farther. So Jesus said if you overcome, if you do what I tell you to do, you get your eyesight restored. You get your counsel from me and you overcome, and I will grant of you to come up hither. He wants to give us a spiritual vantage point by which we are able to see more clearly what God is doing in our lives.

If we are living down here so far beneath the promises, the principles, the power, the authority, the anointing and the victories of God, it's going to be hard for us to trust in truthful reality isn't it. Instead we'll put our confidence in the natural. But the Lord says, let's restore your vision, come on up here, get intimate with me. Intimacy with God restores our spiritual vision.

If you come up here with me and get intimate with me as I am seated at the throne of God where power and authority and victory are, you are going to be seeing things the way they really are. You will see truth, victory, and you will become a triumphant Christian.

But we've got to get up there. How do we do that? First we see ourselves as Jesus sees us, wretched, poor, naked, and blind.

Now, I cry out again to the Christians that are like the sons of Issachar, those that understand the times, the remnant that can discern who their brothers and sisters are as they hear HIS Word. This is the remnant that seeks the leadership of Shepherds:

- Shepherds who have denied themselves

- Shepherds who have picked up their cross and follow Jesus

- Shepherds who will die for their flock

- Shepherds who love God with all their heart, mind, soul and strength and will stand in harm's way for the innocent

- Shepherds that are pious, while teaching only as the true shepherd teaches by bearing witness to the Truth, no matter the cost

- Shepherds who stand, contending for the faith

- Shepherds who bend their knee only to Christ

- Shepherds who kneel down and pray, then repeat Christ's words, "not my will, but thy will be done" then get up off of their knees and take action by leading to the cross

Because of the lack of True Shepherds, our children's lives and souls are at risk. Our families are at risk, and our country is at risk. May Jesus chastise them because of His love for them, and may He forgive their Pride, Disobedience, Fear, Greed, Silence, and yes even Willful Ignorance. May each Shepherd seek to love God with all of their heart, mind, soul and strength, and truly love their brothers as they love themselves. Let the Shepherds take hold of their flock and lead them out of the wilderness caused by the pulpits of our land.

Lord, we bow our knees before You, please change the hearts and actions of our Shepherds to be servants for your honor and glory and protectors of your flock, or eliminate them in some way, so they cause no further harm to your sheep.

Jesus said, *"you are either with me or against me, you either gather with me or you scatter"* (Luke 11:23).

Aborted States in America

35

WHERE ARE THE PROPHETS?

A.W. Tozer gives some insights into the need to get away from what many preachers, pastors, and priests are doing today, because of a need for some prophetic preachers.

"If Christianity is to receive a rejuvenation, it must be by other means than any now being used. If the Church in the second half of this century is to recover from the injuries she suffered in the first half, there must appear a new type of preacher. The proper, ruler-of-the-Synagogue type will never do. Neither will the priestly type of man who carries out his duties, takes his pay and asks no questions, nor the smooth-talking pastoral type who knows how to make the Christian religion acceptable to everyone. All these have been tried and found wanting.

Another kind of religious leader must arise among us. He must be of the old prophet type, a man who has seen visions of God and has heard a voice from the Throne. When he comes (and I pray God there will be not one but many), he will stand in flat contradiction to everything our smirking, smooth civilization holds dear. He will contradict, denounce and protest in the name of God and will earn the hatred and opposition of a large segment of Christendom. Such a man is likely to be lean, rugged, blunt-spoken and a little bit angry with the world. He will love Christ and the souls of men to the point of willingness to die for the glory of the One and the salvation of the other. But he will fear nothing that breathes with mortal breath.

This is only to say that we need to have the gifts of the Spirit restored again to the Church. And it is my belief that the one gift we need most now is the gift of prophecy.

"Of the sons of Issachar who had understanding of the times, to know what Israel ought to do, their chiefs were two hundred" (1 Chr 12:32). A prophet is one who knows his times and what God is trying to say to the people of his times.

Today we need prophetic preachers; not preachers of prophecy merely, but preachers with a gift of prophecy. The word of wisdom is missing. We need the gift of discernment again in our pulpits. It is not ability to predict that we need, but the anointed eye, the power of spiritual penetration and interpretation, the ability to appraise the religious scene as viewed from God's position, and to tell us what is actually going on.

Where is the man who can see through the ticker tape and confetti to discover which way the parade is headed, why it started in the first place and, particularly, who is riding up front in the seat of Honor?

What is needed desperately today is prophetic insight. Scholars can interpret the past; it takes prophets to interpret the present. Learning will enable a man to pass judgment on our yesterdays, But it requires a gift of clear seeing to pass sentence on our own day.

"Lord, I pray for that gift of prophetic insight. Move me beyond the knowledge You've enabled me to gain through education, reading, and study. I pray that I might lead as one 'who has seen visions of God and has heard a voice from the throne.' Amen."

Lord help us! Hopefully the priests, pastors, and ministry leaders will be convicted to pray that God will give them the wisdom and courage to deny themselves and lead their flocks as Jesus would. Lord give us Shepherds that will answer your call, so that the sheep will not be scattered, yet like Mother Theresa said, "don't wait on the leaders."

We must have Biblical obedience and continue to do good, even if our Shepherds lack the Masculine Christianity to lead and protect.

Father change the Shepherds heart and walk for Christ or eliminate them and raise up some new ones that are men after your heart, in Jesus' name, Amen.